THE PRE-HISTORY OF THE ARMENIANS

VOLUME · 1

GABRIEL SOULTANIAN

THE PRE-HISTORY OF THE ARMENIANS

VOLUME · 1

BENNETT & BLOOM

First published in 2003
by Bennett and Bloom
PO Box 2131
London W1A 5SU
England
www.bennettandbloom.com

© Gabriel Soultanian 2003

Typeset and designed by Desert♥Hearts
Maps by Gabriel Soultanian
Additional graphics by Bill Greenwood

Printed and bound by
Newton Printing, London, England

British Library Cataloguing in Publication Data
A catalogue record for this book is available from the British Library

ISBN 1 898948 24 0 (paperback)
ISBN 1 898948 25 9 (hardback)

Dedicated to the memory of
MOVSES KHORENATSI

"Tigran extended the borders
of our country (Armenia)
up to the edge of our
habitation places
in antiquity."
—Khorenatsi, Book I.24

CONTENTS

MAPS

ILLUSTRATIONS & TABLES

PREFACE

Caucasian studies have advanced greatly within the last forty years. Many scholars (far too many to list here) have devoted their efforts to these investigations. With regard to Armenia, its Urartian heritage is now well documented, but the history of the Hay component of its heritage remains largely speculative, since the various existing accounts lack any secure factual basis. It was my dissatisfaction with this state of affairs that prompted my own studies in the hope of discovering the true pre-history of the Hays. I have always believed that these people, speaking as they did an Indo-European language, must have originated from outside of Anatolia.

This book is an account of my findings, based both on Armenian and other sources. Some of the latter — but not as many as I would have liked — are impeccable, and when combined with the Armenian sources, offer, I believe, the possibility of an essentially correct account of the evolution of the Armenian nation.

I am grateful to all the past scholars who have worked on this subject. My paticular indebtedness and gratitude go to Movses Khorenats'i, J. D. Hawkins and I. L. Merker. I am also exceedingly grateful to Ralph Herdan for his encouragement and help with the English language. Finally, my thanks go to my publisher, Nicholas Awde, for his enthusiasm and hard work.

Gabriel Soultanian
Marple Bridge

Hayk
(Eshpai)

INTRODUCTION

Masters of the Highlands

The ethnonym Armenian, meaning the people of Aram, was created in the sixth century BC in order to distinguish a new people speaking an Indo-European language, who entered Urartu circa 590 BC and eventually became the masters of the highlands. The word Armenian, being a foreign appellation, is used only by non-Armenians; it does not exist in the vocabulary of these people who, since times immemorial, have called themselves 'Hay', which means a 'titan' and a 'giant'; though, some ancient writers of the Classical Armenian period have also used the appellations 'Aramian', 'Haygazian' and even 'Askanazian'.

These people originated in the central Balkans, where they were known by such names as Pelagonians, Paeonians, Laioi, Paioplai and so on. All the names of these various clans appear in Greek but, as will be seen later, when their derivations are explained they confirm that the people referred to were all of Hay stock.

The Armenians, in their own language, still call themselves 'Hay' and their country 'Hayastan'. It may become confusing to assign this autonym, which has been in use for such a long time, to different periods; therefore, in the following pages for the sake of clarity whenever these people are referred to, I will use the appellation 'proto-Armenian' for the period before the sixth century BC and 'Armenian' after that date. The Hay autonym will seldom be used.

Genesis of the proto-Armenians

The Armenian nation is of mixed origins. The two main peoples involved in the making of the Armenian nation were the indigenous 'Urartians' and the 'Hays',[1] newcomers (circa 590 BC), speaking an Indo-European dialect.

Around the beginning of the sixth century BC, the disintegrating kingdom of Urartu had come to an end at the hands of Scytho-Median forces and the entire country faced ruin and conquest. The proto-Armenians, moving eastwards from the country of Aram in Anatolia, and in concert with the Urartians, invaded the highlands. With the help of the remnants of the Urartian army, they defeated the Scytho-Median forces,[2] as we shall see later.

From this time onwards the proto-Armenians were called 'Arminã' by the Persians and a little later the Greek geographer Hecataeus called them 'Armenoi'. The indigenous people of Urartu did not migrate to other countries or vacate their habitations (there is evidence that they stayed) and the two peoples, in time, merged into a single nation which became known as Armenia and its people, Armenians.[3] The resulting population was in the main, like the Urartians, of Caucasian physical type, but the language that prevailed was that of the proto-Armenians, the Indo-European newcomers. The language of the proto-Armenians was well constructed and expressive,[4] but the most important reason for its success was the fact that their migrations into the new country Urartu was in waves spread over a period of 400 years.

In this book I shall not deal with the Urartian side of the Armenian people. Urartian history, as well as their Hurrian beginnings,[5] are presently well documented.[6] Furthermore, the history of the Armenians after the fifth century BC will not be a part of this study. My purpose is to prove that the proto-Armenians, the Indo-European core of the Armenian nation, were migrants from the Balkans, and to give an account of their whereabouts and activities from the time they left the Balkans, until the time they were named Armenians.

A history of theories

Up to the end of World War II the history textbooks used in schools would claim that the Armenians came from Thrace. This theory was based on the teachings of the learned monks of the Mkhitarist Order from the Armenian monastery on the island of St. Lazzaro in Venice.[7] One of the authors of this theory was Dr. M. Chamchian, whose much-acclaimed classic three volume work on Armenian history was published in 1784-86.[8]

Chamchian had based the ethnogenesis part of his work on Movses Khorenatsi's *History of the Armenians*, which was a work of the second half of 5th century AD.[9] But Chamchian enlarged on certain themes and included many details that have no historical foundation. For instance, Chamchian's chronology, in respect to the many names Khorenatsi gives in Book 1, Chapters 10-22, was based on counting generations, and he also assumed a father-to-son succession of rulership. Both are impossible to reconcile with historical facts, because fifty-odd names of rulers would require a period of at least a millennium. It is well established that the Orontid dynasty, which is not included in the name-lists, starts at the end of the 5th century BC. In other words, there is not enough time for all these rulers to have existed in Armenia. In Chamchian's work one must take account of his particular religious perspective, and equally in that of Khorenatsi. They were both clerics

In Khorenatsi's history, the basis of the Thracian derivation was the Armenian tradition that T'orgom (Togarmah) was the father of Hayk. In the biblical book of Genesis it is stated that Togarmah was a son of Gomer.[10] However, Gomer was not a progenitor of the Thracians, whereas Tiras, the youngest son of Japhet (Noah's first born) probably was.[11] In order to reconcile the Armenian tradition with that of the Bible, Khorenatsi slightly changes the genealogy of Japhet's progeny by making Tiras a son of Gomer, whereby Togarmah becomes the son of Tiras and father of Hayk.

Records of the ancient chroniclers

There are at present three competing theories concerning the origins of the Armenians. I shall briefly discuss these in the following pages. But first it would be of interest to see what some of the ancient historians and geographers have to say about the Armenians.

The first Greek to use the ethnonym Armenian was Hecataeus of Miletus, who was a Persian official and must have heard the appellation from his superiors. Therefore the Persians must have been using the ethnonym 'Arminã' ('Armināiã' in Aramaean) some time before its appearance in the Bisitun (Behistun) inscriptions of Darius I (522-486 BC).[12]

Herodotus in his Histories (Vll.73) comments on the similarity of Armenian attire, weaponry and language to that of the Phrygians, and concludes that the Armenians were Phrygian colonists. The observations of Herodotus are in no way surprising, in view of my finding that the Armenians, prior to entering Anatolia, were called Paeonians, which makes them neighbours to the Phrygians while in the Balkans, as they had been while in Anatolia.

Eudoxus (c. 370 BC), as quoted by Stephanus Byzantinus in his Ethnica, refers to the Armenian and Phrygian common origin and says that the languages spoken by them were similar.[13]

Strabo (63 BC-25 AD) says that the two Thessalian historians, Cyrsilus of Pharsalia and Medius of Larissa, who wrote the ancient history of Armenia at the court of Seleukos Nikator in Antiochia,[14] asserted that the original country of the Armenians was Thessaly. Strabo also concludes that the progenitor of the Armenian people was a certain Armenus[15] who came from Thessaly and that after him his progeny became known as Armenoi.[16] Thessaly was near enough to Paeonia, but Armenus the Argonaut giving his name to the Armenians is somewhat far-fetched. Armenus is an Indo-European word, whereas Arminã, Armināiã and Armenian are not. The stem of Arminã is Arm, the shortened version of Aram. Armenus has more to do with 'armenizo' (to set sail [?]), more befitting to an Argonaut.

Flavius Josephus in his *Antiquities of the Jews* (Complete Works, Book I.VI.4), tells us that Aram had four sons of whom Ul (~ Hul) somehow personified the Armenians through a town bearing his name. I do not know where this town was, unless its name is a variant of 'Hulmeru', of 'Qullameri/ Qilmeru', which was later renamed Chlomaron by the Romans and Gełimar by the Armenians. The important information in this statement, which is in concordance with the traditions of the Armenians that they were sons of Togarmah (Togarmah was a city of Aram), is the Aram connection. This statement makes the Armenians one of the people who evolved in Aram (south-eastern Anatolia).

**The proto-Armenians are the
Paeonian people of the Balkans**

As already noted, Herodotus considers the Armenians a Phrygian related people. But Strabo attributes the same origins to the Paeonians.[17] The Armenians themselves claim Balkan (Thracian) origins. These attributions appear to support the linguistic theory that during the middle of the second millennium BC the Armenians dwelt in the Balkans, because the Armenian language shows strong Balkan affinities.[18]

Moreover, several linguists of the 20th century, who had studied the Armenian language, had come to the conclusion that the proto-Armenians were Paeonians.[19] They based their arguments on the 'Pai' (transcribed as 'Hay') of the ethnonym 'Paeonian' in addition to certain Illyrian names such as Paio, Paius, and Thracian names containing the 'Pai' stem, such as Παης and Παιβης.[20] Unfortunately, these linguists failed to explain the word Paeonian because they derived the Παι/'Hay' stem from the Indo-European **'pei', 'poi' or 'pou', meaning 'small' or 'pastoralists-herdsmen'.[21] We do not have any

Paeonian words to compare with those of Classical Armenian. All the Paeonian names from the Balkans have reached us through Greek. The Paeonians did not have their own script.

As far as the theory of Paeonian and Armenian relationship is concerned the above remarks represent the state of knowledge up to the present. From this point on, I shall rely on my own researches.

The Armenians are the remnants of the Khayashan people

After the end of World War II information about the Hittites began to appear in profusion, and with it came the knowledge of a country, to the east of the Hittites, known as Azzi Khayasha.[22] This nebulous kingdom was alternatively ruled by princes of Azzi and Khayasha[23] and what we know of it derives solely from the Hittite inscriptions. The word Khayasha may mean the country of the Khays. Khay sounds similar to the autonym of the Armenians, except that, instead of the glottal h sound it uses the uvular χ (kh). It is, however, true that the Van dialect of the Armenian language used the *χay* (*khay*) pronunciation against the universal *hay*,[24] which phenomenon has an historical explanation. Van (Tushpa), the capital city and its surroundings, were the stronghold of Urartu, where the concentration of the indigenous people was higher than elsewhere. This might be the reason why the Urartian χ/kh pronunciation prevailed.[25]

This *Khay* in *Khay*asha prompted many Armenian scholars, in the absence of any other concrete evidence, to study everything available relating to Khayasha and come up with the theory that the Armenians were the remnants of that kingdom and country. In particular, S. T. Eremyan's, and for that matter G. A. Łapantsyan's theories too, are very subtle, though far-fetched. Very briefly this theory has it that the people of the disintegrated kingdom of Khayasha, during the population upheavals of the 12th century BC, migrated south in the guise of the Urumean people[26] to Shubria, where, intermingling with the indigenous population and the Mushki, one of the Sea People's congolomerates, they evolved to nationhood speaking a Thraco-Phrygian dialect. It was this ethnic unity that was called Arime by Adad-nirari II (911-891 BC) and Arme by Sarduri II (764-735 BC).[27] Of course, this theory and its elaborations influenced western historians, too. To mention two, Toumanoff and Lang, who develop the theory by introducing an element of the Indo-European language by postulating a Phrygian (Mushki) and Khayashan intermingling (ignoring the Urumeans), whereby the Indo-European language prevails. It appears that these scholars have ignored the fact that after the 14th century one never comes across references to Khayasha again; even though the Hittite inscriptions continued for another century. Moreover, by the turn of the millennium, in the place where Khayasha used to be we find a new Hurrian kingdom of Daiene (Diauhe).

There was also a serious attempt to explain some Khayashan divine, personal, and place names, in reconstructed Indo-European stem words, which gave a spurious support to the theory on linguistic grounds.[28] Thereafter, this theory became, for a short time, the mainstay of Armenian ethnogenesis studies. On certain linguistic grounds it was conjectured that there were some correlations, though these correlations were not universally accepted.

Only five regnal names are known from Khayasha (I ignore god and place names which are usually transmitted from one nation to another). These are Annias, Marias, Aissias, Khukkana and Muttis; there is also another, doubtful due to the illegibility of the inscription. Scholars give this sixth name as Karanis or Lannis. Of these names Khukkana can be compared with Bitkhana of Khussara and Annias can be compared with Anittas, the son of Bitkhana and the first king of Kanesh. But, there was also an Anita, recorded in 2540 BC, who was the cup-bearer of Ur-Nanshe (c. 2550 BC), king of Lagash in Sumer.

It appears these names belong to the Hurrian language and

have nothing of Armenian provenance, because there seems to be no link between Khayasha and the Armenians, which is not the case with the Hurrian and Neo-Hurrian (Urartian) languages.[29] It is also notable that in Armenia, ancient or modern, there is no place name ending with a 'sha' suffix as in Khayasha, which is found in westernmost Asia Minor.

The Armenian plateau used to be the homeland of the Hurrian people where in the 9th century BC the kingdom of Urartu was born. The languages of Urartu and that of the Hurrians have strong affinities.[30] The proto-Armenians lived from the 12th century to the 6th to the west and south-west of Urartu before entering the country which, in the course of the 6th century BC, became known as Armenia. This means that the proto-Armenians were immediate neighbours of Urartu for six centuries. In the course of these six centuries the proto-Armenians cohabitated with the Hurrian people in Aram (south-eastern Anatolia), which may explain the prevailing Hurrian words in the Armenian language. After the sixth century the assimilation of the highland peoples, (the proto-Armenians, Urartians, Hurrians, Mardians, etc) provided the Armenian language with many local words and suffixes, which were in addition to those already borrowed from the Hurrians of Aram. This may explain why the Armenian language has a strong substratum older than Classical Armenian.[31]

Finally, it is odd that one never comes across the name Hay or Armenian in any ancient inscription between the collapse of Khayasha and the time (6th century BC) the ethnonym Arminã was created. It is also remarkable that the language of the Hurrians and the Urartians contain no Armenian words, whereas the reverse is true of the Armenian language.

**The Armenians are the indigenous
people of the Armenian highlands**
Within the last 30 to 40 years a number of young Armenian historians decided that the Armenians were the indigenous

highland people of the country. Initially this theory sounded contradictory, far-fetched and even sensational until V. Ivanov and T. Gamkrelidze published their paper in 1981 on the problem of the homeland and migrations of the Indo-Europeans.[32] Their new findings gave support to the claim of indigenous origin, although the theory was questionable on historical grounds and as a solution to the homeland problem, wholly without archaeological support.[33]

For our purposes, it does not matter whether the Armenian highlands were the original homeland of Indo-Europeans or not. One thing however can be said. If the Indo-Europeans migrated out of these highlands, the proto-Armenians, too, must have been a part of that movement. For in the Armenian language there are many Finno-Ugric and Baltic loan words, making it difficult to account for these northern loan words[34] had the proto-Armenians remained in their highlands.

The fusion of this theory of indigenous origin with that of Khayashan derivation soon followed, a refinement which gave the new combined theory a semblance of true history; even though the support from Ivanov and Gamkrelidze was controversial.[35]

According to O. R. Gurney, the evidence from excavations and examination of skulls found on relevant sites show that in the third millennium the majority of the population of Anatolia were dolichocephalic. In the second millennium, the brachycephalics account for 50 per cent, but in neither millennium are the hyper-brachycephalics with flattened occiput (Armenoid type) to be found. It was only in the first millennium BC that the Armenoid type appeared.[36]

The objections I raised in the last paragraph of the previous section, namely that there is no supporting evidence for a Khayashan derivation, and that the Hurrian and Urartian languages do not have Armenian loan words, whereas the opposite is true of the Armenian language,[37] are just as valid in the case of the indigenous origin theory.

In support of the indigenous origin theory one hears of Armanum/Armani (deriving from the inscription of Naram-Sin [2251-2215 BC] of Agade), which by a miracle becomes part of the Armenian highlands. This is too far-fetched to deserve comment.

The obscure appellation of 'Arme' in an inscription of Sarduri II of Urartu remains open to various interpretations unless it is a scribal mistake or, more likely, a reference to the Aramaeans of around Amed. Whatever the explanation, it is important to note that this 'Arme' occurs in an inscription of the mid-eighth century BC so there is nothing really ancient about it to warrant investigation for the roots of the proto-Armenians. The previous monarchs of Urartu could not have ignored the existence of such a country, particularly if it was within the highlands, and certainly the Assyrians would have known of, and recorded the existence of such a country on their northern borders.[38]

It is apparent that neither the theory of the Khayashan derivation, nor the one of indigenous origin, is supported by any historical evidence. They are the creations of various scholars to fill the gap in our knowledge of the ethnogenesis of the Armenian people.

PART I

CHAPTER 1

THE PAEONIANS

Sun worshippers and gods

Linguists, in the main, assert that the Armenian people during the middle of the second millennium BC must have dwelt in the Balkans,[39] where they were known as the Paeonians. Unfortunately, our knowledge of the Paeonians, before the time of Herodotus (circa 5th century BC), is so sparse that to give an account of them requires considerable conjecture and inference.

The source materials that we have to hand consist of a few statements concerning the Paeonian migrations into Anatolia and what Homer says in the *Iliad*. Even this meagre selection, in the case of Homer, is controversial.

The limited archaeological excavations conducted by Yugoslavian and Greek scholars are not sufficient to form an image of the Paeonian cultural background, nor do these investigations furnish us with definitive ethnic identities or tribal affiliations, because any information so obtained with regard to the Paeonians, is no more than a by-product of their primary objectives, which are Macedonian and Illyrian studies.

The Paeonian language, again, remains unaccountable because our knowledge amounts to nothing, but for a single word, which Aristotle had recorded in his *Historia Animalium* (630a) as 'monapos', meaning a European bison. The classical geographer of the Armenian period, Anania Shirakatsi (7th century AD) mentions the same word as 'bonos'[40] without referring to Paeonia, but Adjaryan in his *Dictionary of Armenian Root Words* has

The Central Balkans and the Paeonian settlements
(12th–8th centuries B.C.)

Strymon
MUSOI
MEDICE
R. Nestus
THRACIA
SINTICE
ODOMANTIS
SIRIOPAEONIANS
DOBERES
BISALTIA
gaeon
ESTONIA
EDONIS
PAEOPLAI
NIA
Abdera
M. Pan
L. Bolbe
Thasos
erme
Gulf of
Strymon
Samothrace
HALCIDICE
Sithonia
Imbros
M. Athos
Pallene
Troy
erme
Lemnos
AEGEAN SEA
os
Lesbos

it as 'bonosos', with a claim that it is a loan from Greek.

According to Maximus of Tyre,[41] a writer of the second century AD, the Paeonians were sun worshippers, which is confirmed from the proto-Armenian inscriptions of Aram, circa 10th to 7th centuries BC. But sun worship was only one of the facets of the Paeonian/proto-Armenian religion, which, both in the Balkans and Anatolia also had other gods. The chief god of their pantheon in Paeonia was Tyr, an ancient Indo-European name for Zeus.[42] The other god name we know of was Thyales/Dyales, identified with Dionysos.[43] It appears that of these two gods, Thyales was a later acquisition, perhaps from the Thracians. Neither of these gods is commemorated in any of the proto-Armenian inscriptions of Aram, where the Paeonians or the proto-Armenians had settled from the 12th to the 6th centuries BC, prior to entering Urartu. One aspect of their religion that we note from the said inscriptions was the fact that fire was holy and was procured by the priestly caste.[44]

It is remarkable that Tyr remained one of the gods of the Armenian pantheon up to the time of the adoption of Christianity. He was the scribe god of ecstasy (inducer of dreams), poetry and magic, usually equated with Hermes. Though, one might think that Tyr's attributes were closer to those of the Scandinavian god Odin (Anglo-Saxon Woden/Wotan), and yet it was the Teutonic god Tew who was also known by the name of Tyr.[45]

With the Achaemenid conquest and domination of Armenia a new religious order was imposed, wherein Ahura Maxda was the chief god and Tyr his scribe. As for Thyales, his orgasmic aspect was transferred to the goddess Anahida, after which we lose sight of him.

Settlers of Pelagonia

Sometime during the second half of the third millennium BC the proto-Armenians had arrived and settled in the highlands of the later Pelagonia. With the turn of the millennium, invaders from the north, speaking a version of what later became the

Greek language,[46] followed the proto-Armenian example, but they overtook them settling in the Peloponnese and parts of the mainland Greece. This first wave of the Helladic people became known as the later Mycenaeans/Achaeans.

From various Finno-Ugric and Baltic loan words in the vocabulary of the Armenian language[47] it can be hypothesized that the proto-Armenians, too, had come to Pelagonia from the north. Further support in this connection comes from the name of their chief god Tyr, who was one of the older gods of the Teutonic pantheon.[48] In the Balkans, Tyr was exclusive to the Paeonians and later to the Armenians of Armenia.

Encroachment of the Pelagonian lands by the Brygi or Brygians, a Phrygian related people, began in the 13th century BC — this date is based on archaeological excavations of the cemeteries at Pazhok, which were dated to 1300 to 700 BC.[49] These people had come from the east and as Herodotus (VII.73) tells us, held the lakelands of Pelagonia for many centuries. As a rule the Lausitz culture is ascribed to the Brygians.

The pressure on the Pelagonians increased in the 12th century BC when a new wave of the Helladic people, known as the Dorians, advanced from the north, which forced the Pelagonians to expand to the east. It seems, this was the time when the new ethnonym of 'Paeonian' was created by the Greeks. Paeonian means 'Hay creatures' (Παι-ον-ες), which, like 'barbarian', reflects the Greek low opinion of non-Greek people. It was the Greeks in the first place who had named the Hays, settled to the east of Lake Lychnidus (present-day Ohrid), 'Pelagonians', which means 'Assembly of Hays' (Πελ–αγων–ες).

It appears, the Greeks knew the meaning of the word 'Hay', which they did not translate, because such a translation would have been rather confusing, considering that their first gods were called the Titans, and 'hay' means 'titan' and 'giant', which Strabo knew centuries later, as in Book VII.40 where he says that "the Titans too were called Pelagonians". I think Homer, too, knew this fact, which is evident from the words he puts into the mouth of Asteropaeus in *Iliad* XXI.179-80 as "the Pelegon begot, the spear-renown'd of Pelegon I boast me sprung."[50] In the second half of the 8th century BC due to Macedonian pressure on the lands previously occupied by the Paeonians, a migration to the east of the River Strymon towards the Pangaeon Mountains started, when new tribal names started to emerge. This period may also be the time when the migrant Paeonians attacked the city of Perinthus[51] on the northern coast of Propontis (present Sea of Marmara).

Names in Homer's epics

Homer's *Iliad* is an important source for this study. Scholars, who have studied and analysed it, have concluded that it is devoid of history, which is not altogether convincing, as there is much in the *Iliad* that they use for their own purposes.

Nevertheless, Homer in both of his books, the *Iliad* and the *Odyssey*, is not writing history but epic poems which require figurative and parabolic language in order to keep the listeners spellbound. Strabo (I.2.9) says that "Homer took a historical fact and decked it up with his myths", which, I believe, sounds plausible. But there is much more to Homer than that. The *Iliad*, particularly, has vast amount of valuable information that one cannot afford to overlook because Homer is the first to mention Troy and the Trojan War, the Achaeans, Phrygians, Paeonians, Mysians, Thracians, etc. He was also the first to mention geographical localities (albeit with a few errors), personal names, some of which have since been confirmed, the ancient Greek pantheon and so on.

This part of this study is concerned with two of his more astonishing names (Nestor's cup or similar disclosures do not form part of this study), those of Pyraechmes and Asteropaeus. How could Homer know these names? These are two complicated compounds, which rule out coincidence. Scholarship accepts that Homer is emulating older epics of previous bards, in which case the *Iliad* must contain a core of first-hand knowledge of events and personalities cloaked in an ancient oral art form, which is supposed to keep the tradition alive for the benefit of the generations to come. If this reasoning is correct, then, the inference that Homer's account, stripped of myth and parabola, contains a framework of true events.

In the catalogue of the participants in the Trojan War the first contingent of Paeonians were under the leadership of Pyraechmes (*Iliad* 11.981). But the second contingent had arrived only eleven days before the death of their leader Asteropaeus (XXI.172-81). Here are two names of Paeonian leaders translated into Greek:

Pyraechmes ('Pyr-aechmes') means 'flame tip', which in Classical Armenian was recomposed as Zarmayr ('Z-arm-ayr') meaning the same. We do not have the proto-Armenian version of this name.[52]

Asteropaeus means 'flash of lightning' and is the Greek translation of the proto-Armenian name Qatazilu ('Qataz-ilu') meaning 'overflowing with sparks' = 'lightning'. This was the name of the first proto-Armenian king of Kummukh in Aram (south-eastern Anatolia). The Classical Armenian recomposition of this name was Ampak ('Amp-ak') meaning 'source of lightning' = 'lightning', which is the same as the modern word 'kaytsak' ('kayts-ak') meaning 'source of sparks' = 'lightning'.

Of course, Homer gives us many more Greek translations of Paeonian names, for which I do not find any parallels among the names of the proto-Armenian rulers of Aram.

Expansion eastwards

Of the many Paeonian tribes, Homer in the *Iliad* mentions only the Pelagonians and the Paeonians, which fits the chronological pattern, because the period he is describing was before the dispersion of these people. Even the name Paeonian may be a later creation. Pelagonians means 'Assembly of Hays' as we have seen above, and these people were the westernmost settlers living by the lakelands of the central Balkans. They had named the largest lake Lychnidus (present-day Ohrid), a name that would be carried over to Armenia for the present-day Lake Sevan. After their dispersion to what became the later Paeonia, they were renamed as Paeonians. With their later expansion further to the east, to the Strymon valley and the mountains of Pangaeon, they were still known as Paeonians, but some of the tribes were denoted by the names of the districts they lived in.

From later writers we learn the full list of the Paeonian tribes, which included, in addition to the Pelagonians:

Agrianes: These are recorded as soldiers serving in Alexander the Great's army.

Laioi:[53] This name transcribes as Hays,

Mygdonians:[54] These tribes were in central Paeonia. We meet them again in later Armenia, around the city of Nisibis in the new Mygdonia.

Odomantians:[55] We meet them again in the west of Armenia in the new Odomantis, where the kingdom of Zariadres was founded.

Siriopaeonians:[56] These settled in what later became Cappadocia and became known as the *White Syrians*.

Doberes:[57] These were neighbours of the Odomantians and Paeoplai, but due to Thracian pressure had moved to the Axius basin by the 4th century BC.

Paeoplai:[58] This name means 'Hays of the Fringe', as they were the easternmost Paeonian tribe.

The map on page 26 illustrates how these people were dispersed in the Balkans. From the River Nestus in the east to Lake Ohrid to the west; from the source of Morava river in the north to Pieria, taking in the Thermaic Gulf, to the south.[59]

The main river of Paeonia was the Axius, which means 'the worthy'. This river name, too, will be repeated in later Armenia, where the central main river will be named, literally, 'the primary value' = Araxi, which is the same as 'Axi-us'.

In Homer's time, it appears the main city of Paeonia was

Amydon (*Iliad* 11.981); but by the fourth century BC Bylazora, nowadays Titov Veles, had become the capital city. Bylazora has the same meaning as the forgotten place name Bayazed in central Armenia (in a depression west of Mount Ararat). The history of this place is confused, because the Arsacids had a castle on the heights up to the fifth century AD in order to guard the north-south and south-west trade routes. The name of this castle was Daroynk', which in Classical Armenian era took precedence over the name of Bayazed. Though some believe that the place was so called after Sultan Bayazid the First (AD 1354-1403, reigned 1389-1402). Turkish sources confirm that Bayazed city existed before his time.[60] It will be useful to see what these place names mean.

Bylazora ('Byl-az-ora') means — 'lair of the fire watchers' and is the Grecised form of the place name Bayazed ('Bay-az-ed'), which means – 'lair before the fire". To understand why such complicated compounds were created one has to look to the geographical locations of the two cities.

Bylazora, the present Titov Veles, lies in the valley of the upper Axius river, between mountains of some 2,000 to 2,500 feet. It was on the north-south trade route and the gateway to Paeonia, Macedonia and Greece. Perhaps, the fire is supposed to represent the barbarians whose hordes used this route in order to attack the southern countries. Therefore, the city was perceived as the guardian of the south, watching over the hordes from the north. Bayazed lies in a depression west of Mount Ararat, surrounded by high mountains, which form a natural buffer zone of difficult access. It was on the west-south and north-south crossroad of trade routes. Its position explains why the migrant Paeonians of Bylazora chose this place and at the same time perpetuated the name of their city they had left behind in the Balkans. Other important cities of Paeonia, according to Thucydides (11.100) were: Atalanta, Europus and Gordynia. The last name we shall see again in Armenia after the migration of its people, as their new settlement areas between the time of Xenophon's *Anabasis* and the battle of Gaugamela in the south of Armenia, which was renamed Gordyene after their city of Gordynia left behind in the Balkans.

The Paeonians defy the Persian Empire
Herodotus, at the beginning of Book V of his histories, recounts a battle between the Paeonians from along the River Strymon and the city of Perinthus on the northern coast of Propontis. He says that this battle took place a long time before Megabazos, Darius I's (522-486 BC) commander, had conquered Perinthus.

Around 512 BC, Darius instructed Megabazos to remove the Paeonians living to the east of the Strymon into Anatolia. The Paeonians had heard of this plan and their forces had gathered on the sea-coast route in order to face the Persian army. Megabazos had intelligence of what was happening and with the help of local guides changed to an overland route, and finding the Paeonian towns empty of fighting men took possession of them (Herodotus, Book V). The Persians managed to round up the Siriopaeonians, the Paeoplai and some other tribes as far as Lake Prasias, but the Paeonians who lived near Mount Pangaeon and the lake were not affected. To explain why Darius decided to remove the Paeonians, Herodotus tells us an amusing story of two brothers, Pigres and Mantyes, and their sister (V.12-17). As for the deportations to Anatolia one might conjecture that there might have been a serious design to remove the obstacle of the Paeonians, who might have been in the way of Darius' objective, which was the conquest of Greece.

In the course of the fifth century BC the Thracian expansion and pressure in the east had forced the Paeonians of the fringe, such as the Doberes, to move to the valley of the River Axius, to the north of the Macedonians. This is where Thucydides (11.96, 98) places them before the Peloponnesian War.

Herodotus also describes how the lake-dwelling Paeonians built their huts. Long piles were driven into the lake, which supported platforms connected to each other by narrow bridges.

Each hut had a trap door to the waters below, which had an abundance of fish. Of these fish he names two; the paprax and the tilon. The word 'paprax' may be of Paeonian origin; perhaps, it is the later Classical Armenian 'papiwk'. Another aspect of Paeonian culture, according to Herodotus, was their polygamous custom which required the man to build a hut for each wife.

By fourth century BC the Paeonian tribal lands to the east of the River Strymon were in the hands of the Thracians. The Siriopaeonians, Paeoplai and the Odomantians had already migrated and settled in Cappadocia and the western parts of Armenia. From this period on, a unified ethnonym of 'Paeonian' under a dynasty of kings is recorded by various writers. However, a few writers still mentioned the Agrianians and the Laioi in order to denote a particular tribe and their achievements.

Beginnings of a kingdom

Unified Paeonia appears to have had wide commercial interests, suggested by finds of various hoards of their silver coins spread over many countries.[61] This fact also implies that a feudal society and a class system was already in existence, which culminated in the establishment of a monarchy. There is a lot we do not know about this kingdom, except for the names of the dynasty, which starts in the first half of the fourth century BC.

The names of the kings of this dynasty were: Agis, Lykpeios, Patraos, Audoleon, Leon and Dropion.

> **Agis**: The date of his succession is not known, but his death falls in 359-8 BC. Soon after the death of Agis, Philip, in 358BC attacked Paeonia in order "to make them obedient to Macedonia". It could well be that the main purpose of Philip's attack had to do with the ownership of the silver mines by Lake Prasias, which used to supply his great-great-grandfather, Alexander, with a talent of silver a day (Herod. V). Philip needed the silver for the organization of his army.

Lykpeios: After a short while Lykpeios succeeded Agis. Neither the date of this succession nor that of his death are known, though he is remembered as one of the anti-Macedonian parties of the Thrace-Illyria-Paeonian alliance of 356 BC. It appears that Lykpeios was the first Paeonian monarch to strike his own silver coins.

Patraos: Possibly succeeded shortly after 331, though this date is again not certain. Like his predecessor he struck his own silver coins and may have died before 310 BC, considering that his successor, Audoleon, was already on the throne by that date. It was during the reign of Patraos that the Paeonian cavalry, lead by Ariston, and the Agrianian foot soldiers were enlisted in Alexander the Great's army. Ariston, the commander of the cavalry succeeded in killing the leader of the Persian horsemen, Satropates,[62] which event was commemorated on the reverse of the silver tetradrachm of Patraos.[63]

Audoleon: Like Patraos and Lykpeios struck his own silver coins, and appears to have died between 284 and 282 BC. His son, Ariston (not to be confused with the commander of the cavalry of Alexander the Great), was the original successor, but due to the treachery of Lysimachus, who annexed Paeonia to Macedonia, on the day of his coronation, and after he had already taken the ritual bath in the River Astibos and was to sit before the ritual table placed for him, he fled to Dardania and was never heard of again.

Leon: He was next on the throne and was, perhaps, another son of Audoleon. From his reign a few bronze coins are preserved, which reflects the depleted wealth of the country; because, beside paying homage to Macedonia, it was early in his reign that in 279 BC Celtic tribes invaded Paeonia, Macedonia and Greece. With the previous migrations the population had already decreased and now another disaster had struck the country. The defeat of the Celts by Antigonus Gonatas in 277 BC forced them to cross into Anatolia, where they settled centrally as the Galataeans. With this repulse of the Celts an uncertain number of Paeonians, too, were driven into Anatolia.[64]

Dropion: Leon was succeeded by his son Dropion, probably about the middle of the third century. Dropion was the last king of the dynasty; an active king, though unfortunately we do not know when and how his rule came to an end. He made dedications to both Delphi and Olympia,[65] which are remembered. Pausanias writes that "King Dropion, son of Leon, dedicated the bronze head of a bison to Delphi" (X.13.1). A second dedication to Delphi of a bronze equestrian statue of Audoleon has the following inscription (this can still be seen): "Dropion, the son of Leon, king of the Paeonians, dedicated this statue of Audoleon his grandfather, according to an oracle, to Pythian Apollo."[66] The dedication to Olympia of a bronze equestrian statue of himself reads: "The Koinon of the Paeonians and king Dropion, son of Leon and founder, dedicated."

It appears that the end of Dropion's rule was either due to the complete depletion of the population of Paeonia or that his death was the reason for the migration of almost the entire population to Anatolia (some moved to the Peloponnese). The migrants who entered Anatolia settled to the south of Armenia, around the city of Nisibis and created the new Mygdonia, but those from Bylazora settled centrally to the south-west of the Ararat mountains and founded the new city of Bayazed.

POPULATION UPHEAVALS AND THE PAEONIANS

The People of the Sea

In the aftermath of the Trojan War, the eastern Mediterranean witnessed immense population upheavals three generations before the inscription of Tiglath-Pileser I (1114-1076 BC) concerning the Mushki. Egypt was under attack by land but mainly by sea, which was the reason why Ramesses III (1184-1153 BC) named the aggressors "the People of the Islands" and "the People of the Sea".[67] There were similar population movements in Anatolia, too, but these were confined to the land within Asia Minor, with reverberations, perhaps, in the surrounding countries. Referring to these unrests, Strabo (12.8.4) says: "Now it was particularly in the time of the Trojan War and after, that invasions and migrations took place, since both the barbarians and the Greeks at that time felt an impulse to acquire possession of the countries of others." Barnett writes that: "The families of the Anatolian migrants followed (the fighting men), partially guarded in wooden ox-driven peasant carts usually of Anatolian type with solid wheels."[68]

As in Egypt, the various tribes involved in the Anatolian population upheavals were also called the People of the Sea, which designation appears to identify them as a part of a grand plan. The only aspects of the Egyptian and Anatolian invasions that were common to both movements were the intention to ransack and steal other peoples' possessions, and their chronology, i.e. they took place at or near the same time.

Scholars usually ascribe these upheavals to famine and climatic changes, and give their accounts of the events starting with the 'movement of the Sea Peoples' or population upheavals. This, considering all the evidence as described in what follows, is untenable because the groups involved in these movements were only small representative contingents from each nation. A famine would not be surprising, as famines were then a regular aspect of life in the eastern Mediterranean (religious groups in these countries still conduct prayer ceremonies for rain). But if famine had been the cause, why was it that only a small number from each nation were on the move, leaving the mass of the population behind in their respective countries, possibly for later migration? In support of this hypotheses one can cite the Thraco-Phrygian conglomerate settled at the confluence of the Euphrates and Arsanias rivers, as the Mushki, or the Urumeans and the Kaskans who had settled around the sources of the Tigris. It took centuries for the Thraco-Phrygian people to cross into Anatolia, whereas, in the case of the Urumeans and the Kaskans they never left their central and western Anatolian lands. The Mycenaeans definitely did not vacate Greece and the islands, except for establishing small colonies on the various seaboards of the Aegean, Mediterranean and Black seas, which were ordinary mercantile expansions, undeterred by any famine.

One might ask how it was that all these wandering people happened to be in a particular place in Anatolia at the same time as if by appointment? When one considers the distances involved in the days of ox-drawn carts without roads one realizes that it was impossible for the Phrygians from the present Albania, Mysians from the present Romania, and the Mycenaeans from the Peloponnese, Crete and the islands, to prearrange a looting expedition in Anatolia. But these people

Anatolia and the Balkans – circa 12th century BC

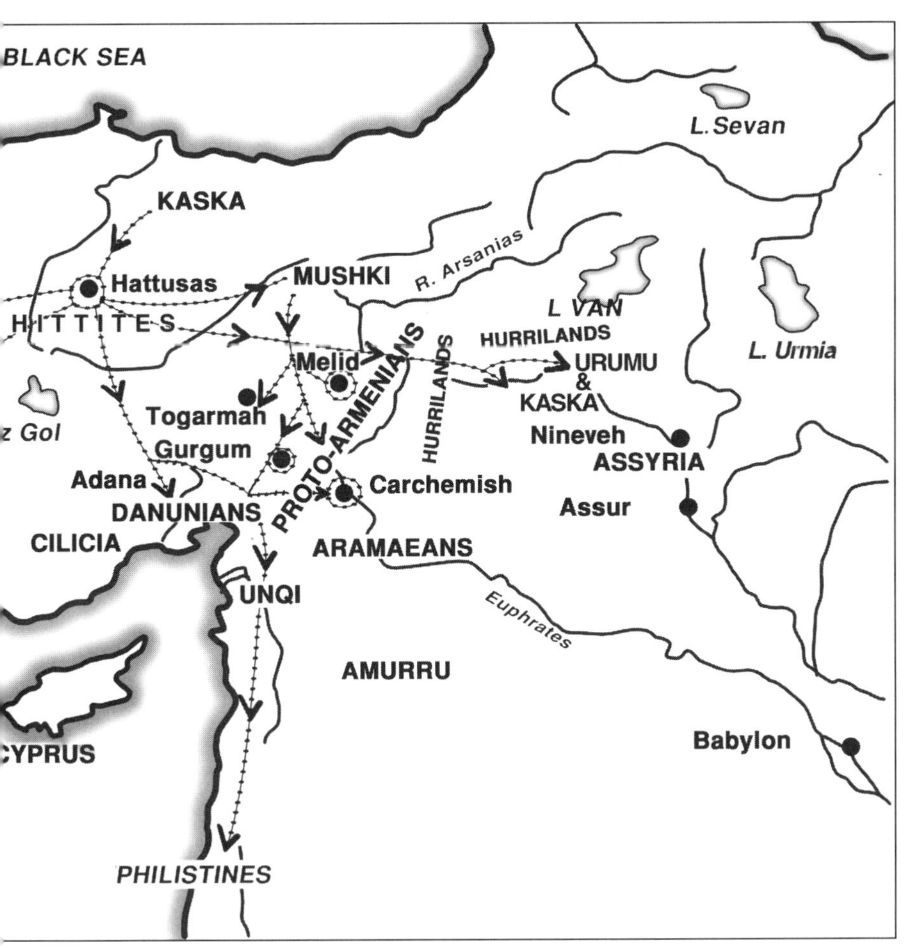
BLACK SEA
L. Sevan
KASKA
R. Arsanias
Hattusas
MUSHKI
L. VAN
HITTITES
HURRILANDS
L. Urmia
Melid
PROTO-ARMENIANS
HURRILANDS
URUMU
&
KASKA
Togarmah
z Gol
Nineveh
ASSYRIA
Gurgum
Adana
Carchemish
Assur
DANUNIANS
PROTO-ARMENIANS
CILICIA
ARAMAEANS
UNQI
Euphrates
AMURRU
CYPRUS
Babylon
PHILISTINES

could have participated in a long-drawn war, arriving at different times, as was the case with Asteropaeus and his men, who had arrived only eleven days before he was killed by Achilles. At the end of the war, all these people would have been on the spot to start their further adventures.

In the aftermath of the Trojan War
Chapter 2 of the *Iliad* details a catalogue of the participants in the Trojan War. If one compares the ethnic names or the localities of these participants with those we know from history as the Sea People an amazing correlation emerges.

After the Trojan War the victorious Mycenaeans, whom Homer calls "Achaeans", "Danaans", "Argives" but seldom "Hellenes", divided into two branches. One branch, with other ethnic groups allied to them for the adventure, went on to attack Egypt by sea, whereas the other branch, a conglomerate of Achaeans, Danaans, Teucrians (all these people were Mycenaeans but the various names given to them became more prominent once they had settled in Palestine) and Paeonians, who had come to Troy under the leadership of Pyraechmes, joined as a coalition — the movement of the Anatolian Sea Peoples. Eventually the Achaeans settled around Gaza and Ascalon. The Teucrians who were probably Cretans settled on the seaboard to the north of them and the Danaans, the Dan of the Bible,[69] settled still further north. Thus the whole old Canaanite seaboard south of Tyre (in present-day Lebanon) became known as Philistia and the people, Philistines (Egyptian Peleset and the Hebrew Pelishtim, though Ezekiel 25:16 and Zephaniah 2:5 call them Cherithites). The Paeonians within this coalition stayed in centres in south-eastern Anatolia, such as Carchemish, Gurgum and Kummukh.[70]

Another coalition among these wandering populations was that of the Urumeans and the Kaskans, who eventually settled at the sources of the River Tigris[71] (the later Armenian Sasoon). The Urumeans were a Luwian-speaking people,[72] whom

Homer calls Lycians. The Kaskans, who had always been to the north of the Hittites,[73] were the natural allies of the Urumeans, as both peoples were eager to see the destruction of the Hittite kingdom, their prime enemy. Perhaps, more than the rest of the wandering populations it was the Kaskans and the Urumeans who dealt the fatal blow to the Hittites. Homer calls the Kaskans "Paphlagonians". Both Lycian and Paphlagonian are later names, but they do indicate the correct geographical locations for the older names, which Homer does not know.

A third group within the Sea Peoples movement became known to the Assyrians as the Mushki, who comprised five tribes.[74] These were the Phrygians, Mysians,[75] Paeonians who had come to Troy under Asteropaeus,[76] the Thracians and the Thessalians (Pelasgians). This group initially settled at the confluence of the Euphrates and Arsanias rivers.[77] All these names appear in the *Iliad*, which records some additional cities whose men participated in the War on the side of the Trojans, because, in the main, they were the neighbours of Priam of Troy. These additional men came from eleven cities. Considering that the distances were not great, it is possible that they returned to their home-towns, or they may have joined a larger related group. The Carians[78] may have joined the Mycenaeans who attacked Egypt and the Maeonians, themselves a Mysian tribe,[79] may have joined their brethren, the Mysians. Homer, in the *Iliad* (II.9.31 & IV.501) makes clear the multitude of the tribes by telling us that "they all spoke different languages".

Ramesses III of Egypt, referring to the Sea People, mentions the "Tjeker", "Shekelesh", "Denyen", "Weshesh", "Meshwesh"[80] and Merneptah, in addition to the previous names, mentions the Lukkans and the Libyans,[81] but it appears neither know of the Kaskans, Urumeans and the Mushki. However, Ramesses' inscription records that Khattusha, Arzawa, Cilicia, Cyprus and Carchemish were all destroyed and the people responsible had set up camp in Amurru.[82]

Tiglath-Pileser I in his inscription[83] mentions all the people Ramesses does not know, and adds that "50 years before his accession (1114 BC) the Mushki were settled in Alzu and Purulumzu", which gives, remarkably, a reciprocal chronology if we compare all the data.

One must not overlook the fact that these wandering people were very slow travellers. They had ox-drawn carts but no roads; they had to stay at a location for at least a year or two in order to sow and reap a harvest and stockpile sufficient food for a few more miles of travel; and, of course, they could not travel at all in the mountainous terrain during the winter snow. To top it all, they had also to fight their passage all the way to their destination.

Movements in Anatolia

The Sea People's invasion of Egypt is not a part of this study, nor that of the Philistines. But various events occurring in Anatolia have to be examined as these are connected to the proto-Armenians and have an influence on their affairs.

Urumeans: It is not known for certain that they were a Luwian-speaking people, nor it is certain that they were the remnants of the disintegrated Arzawan people, the later Lycians. Nevertheless, the root of Urumean is 'uru/ura', which we note is exclusively used by Luwian dialect-speaking Lycians, in such place-names as 'Ura-muus', 'Ura-mu(ua)ta', 'Hura', 'Ouros', the city name of 'Ura' (later Olba in west Cilicia).[84] Tiglath-Pileser I calls these people Hittites, which confirms that they had come from the west. The Urartians, too, called them Hittites, but the country of their settlement Urmie.[85] By the Classical Armenian era these people had assimilated and become known as Armenians, but their language left some traces in the Armenian language, which are referred to as Luwian loan-words[86] — otherwise, the people of Armenia during the classical or later periods had no contacts with any Luwian speakers. It is therefore more than likely that the Urumeans were the remnants of the Arzawan people, whose country, according to Ramesses III, was destroyed during the Anatolian population upheavals.

Kaskans: This ethnonym was known through the inscriptions of the Hittite rulers. The Kaskans of Tiglath-Pileser are qualified with the adjective 'Apeshlaian'.[87] It is not known where this appellation came from; but, considering that the actual name is Kaska, it can be conjectured that they were one of the tribes comprising the Kaska people. Their alliance with the Luwian-speaking Urumeans supports this hypothesis, as both of these people were enemies of the Hittite kingdom. These Kaskans, who had settled with the Urumeans in the later-designated Sasoon mountains, also assimilated and became Armenians by the classical period, though, we cannot say whether their language had left any words in the Armenian vocabulary as we know nothing of it. Tiglath-Pileser calls the Kaskans Hittites too, which makes it clear that they, too, had come from the west.

The western parts of the lands wherein the Urumeans and the Kaskans had subsequently settled, when the proto-Armenians had entered Urartu, became part of the district which the descendants of Tarkunazi (T'ork' Angeł) later claimed.

The origins of the Mushki

The designation 'Mushki' was first recorded by Tiglath-Pileser I, whose inscription, relating to them, reads: "In my accession year 20,000 Mushkis with their five kings, who had held for

50 years the lands of Alzu and Purulumzu . . ."[88] This first reference to the Mushkis should not be confused with that from the time of Sargon II (723-705 BC), because, by the end of the 9th century BC the original Mushkis had ceased to be, and the title was transferred to the newly formed kingdom of Phrygia in central Anatolia. In fact, Ashur-nasir-pal II (883-859 BC) was the last Assyrian monarch who mentions the original Mushkis.

Be that as it may, it is apparent from Tiglath-Pileser's inscription that around 1165 BC a group from the Sea People's conglomerate had arrived and settled at the confluence of the Euphrates and the Arsanias, which lands the Assyrians knew as Alzu and Purulumzu and the people as Mushki.

The name Mushki is the same as the ethnonym 'Musaka'[89] used by the proto-Armenians to denote the Phrygians, as both Mushki and Musaka derive from the stem 'mus', which can also be seen in the city name of Mush to the west of Lake Van.[90] A well-known scholar identifies the original Mushki with the proto-Armenians, which though a speculation contains some truth.[91] The same scholar also tells us that the name Mushki may have been given to these people because the inhabitants of the area had first encountered the Mysians. This is also a conjecture, which, again, appears to contain some truth, but contradicts the identification of the Mushkis with the proto-Armenians.

The proto-Armenian Yarairaisa (Arayan Ara), the caretaker of Carchemish after the death of the ruler Astiruwa (Erast), in his inscription Carchemish A 6.3 (c. 770 BC) refers to both the Mysians and the Phrygians as "Musa-za" and "Musaka-za" respectively. In both cases the stem is 'mus', but it is only in the name of the Phrygians that there is the 'ka' ending which equates with the 'ki' of the Mushki of Assyrian creation. Therefore, the Phrygians were known as Musaka in the proto-Armenian language and Mushki in the Assyrian language. This claim is also supported by the fact that early in 8th century BC the name Mushki was transferred by the Assyrians to the Phrygians of central Anatolia in which event neither the Mysians nor the proto-Armenians had any part.

From the inscription of Tiglath-Pileser it is apparent that the Mushki comprised five tribes, each under its own tribal chief, who the Assyrians call 'kings'. It follows that the Mushki was a coalition of five tribes, i.e. Phrygians, Thracians, Mysians, Paeonians and the Thessalians (Pelasgians). These units being all from the Balkans and neighbours of each other had a similar cultural background, which explains why the whole coalition was designated as Mushki. The number of fighting men, 20,000, that the Mushkis had managed to raise after 50 years of settlement indicates that they were one of the larger groups within the movement of the Sea People of Anatolia, but it is not known whether these new arrivals had any connection with the obscure Mitas of the Hittite records "who was active in the eastern mountains where Khayasha had formerly been."[92]

The Pelagonian Paeonians in the Balkans were the eastern neighbours of the Brygians/Phrygians and throughout their stay in Pelagonia had always participated in various events wherein the Brygians were involved. Even after the complete migration of these two nations it is notable that they settled next to each other in Anatolia; the Brygians/Phrygians centrally and the Pelagonians to the east of them in Tabal.

Anatolia falls to the newcomers

The last group of the Sea Peoples movement in Anatolia that concerns this study was that of the Mycenaeans and the Paeonians, the ones who had first come to Troy under the leadership of Pyraechmes. This group arrived in south-eastern Anatolia by the early 12th century BC; they fought, burned and settled in the main centres.[93] This was the time when a period of "weakness and insignificance" ensued "until the time when they were eventually able to revive a culture."[94]

The image above is part of an illustration of the campaign of Rameses III against Amor (Syria). Note the second prisoner from the left with a medallion and wearing a double-humped turban. The same headgear appears in the picture of an ivory from Megiddo below. The two naked prsioners wearing these headgears are being presented to a Canaanite (?) prince. (From N. K. Sandars, 'The Sea People: Warriors of the Ancient Mediterranean', 1978.)

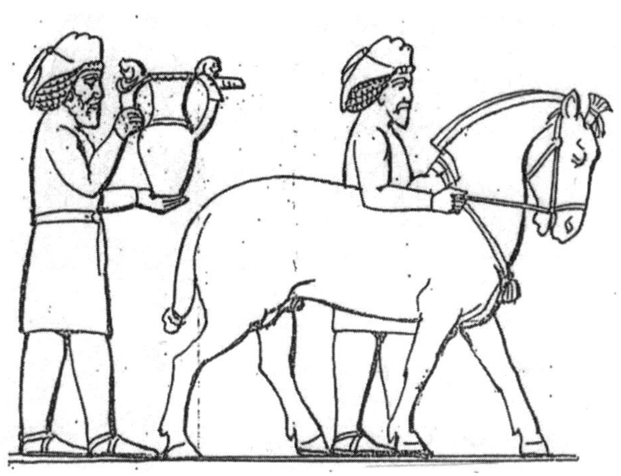

Above is a depiction of Armenian tribute bearers to the court of Darius. These men appear to be wearing a similar headgear seen in the previous pictures. The coin below is that of the Armenian king Xerxes of Tzopk' (Sophene) circa 200 BC. The king's headgear is similar to all the previous ones.

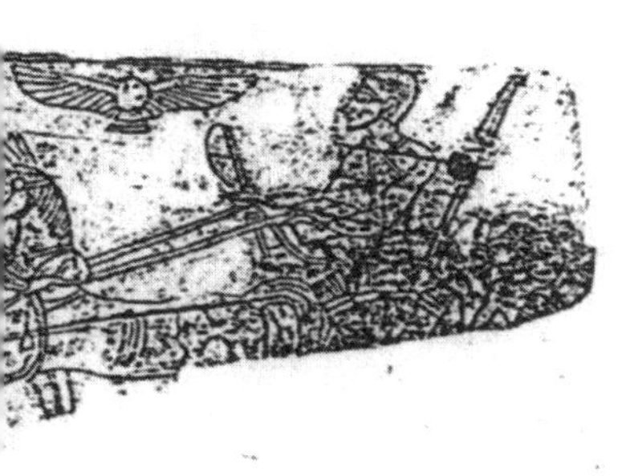

South-eastern Anatolia, known to Armenian traditions as the country of Aram, and Cilicia Campestris were Hurrian countries,[95] and perhaps had a superior cultural background, but they could not match the fighting skills nor cope with the numbers of newcomers. It is also reasonable to expect that the newcomers were much richer in livestock and various other possessions, because, on their way, together with the other groups, they had ransacked, looted and destroyed Khattusha, the capital city, and other places of the Hittite kingdom, which ceased to exist from this time on.

After a few years' respite in south-eastern Anatolia the Mycenaeans were again on the move; this time they were advancing south to the gates of Egypt. At Medinet Habu the inscriptions of Ramesses III (1184-1153 BC) show in relief the arrival of these warlike people with their families protected in ox-drawn carts. It is possible that some Paeonians, too, had joined the Mycenaean move to south, because the reliefs of Medinet Habu show a prisoner with double-humped headgear, corselette and a medallion (figure 1, pp. 50-51). The same headgear is worn, also, by two naked prisoners being presented to a Canaanite? prince on a carved ivory inlay from Megiddo (figure 2). We see the same headgear worn by the Armenian tribute bearers to the court of Darius (figure 3) and on the coin of the Armenian king Xerxes of Tzopk' (Sophene) of around 200 BC (figure 4).

The departure of most of the Mycenaeans to the south had left behind the Paeonians and the Danaans of Cilicia Campestris from around Adana. Of course, the Danaans, too, were Mycenaeans, but considering that history differentiates the various tribes it is possible that they had come from Argos. The Phoenician version of the Karatepe Bilingual of Azatiwata (Norayr of Classical Armenian) call these people 'DNNYM', which must be the Danunim/Denyen/Danaan deriving from the name of Danaos, the king of Argos. Ramesses III mentions the Danaans as the allies of the Philistines.[96]

In the 8th century BC, a kingdom of Adana became prominent, which the Karatepe text calls "the House of Mukasa". Mukasa has been equated with Mopsus[97] of Trojan fame, but in reality there is nothing concrete to connect the two names (there are many persons in Greek traditions with such names), though, it is plausible that Mopsus was the chief of the Danaans when they arrived, and his descendants continued as the House of Mopsus to be the dominant leaders in Adana, where in the 8th century, Awarikus managed to establish a kingdom.

The proto-Armenian Azatiwata (this name means "blazing dawn", meaning "new times", the same as the Classical Armenian recomposition of it as 'Norayr', meaning "new fire") contrary to some conjectures was never a king of Adana, but had become the chief adviser (prime minister) to Awarikus, after whose death he had taken charge of the kingdom until the minor Urikki had come of age and succeeded his father (Azatiwata's inscription will appear in the companion volume of this book in the very near future).

Nevertheless, in the Amarna letters, which belong to the third quarter of the 14th century BC, there is mention of a "Land of Danuna" in a letter written by a certain Abi-milki of Tyre, addressed to Amenophis IV (Akhenaten 1350-1334 BC)[98] and in the 11th century, Ashur-nasir-pal I (11047-1029 BC) of Assyria claims to have defeated the land of Danuna. These two mentions of Danuna are roughly 150 years before and as many years after the arrival of the Danaans into south-eastern Anatolia and Cilicia. Göetze places this particular Danuna in the Turkish district Hatay,[99] which makes sense considering that Hatay had one of the best natural harbours (the Gulf of Alexandretta or Iskenderun) in the east Mediterranean. Therefore, it is conceivable that the Argives of the 14th century BC already had a trading colony in these parts of south-eastern Anatolia, which may have even been the reason why the Danaans of Mopsus stayed behind in Cilicia Campestris.

The Paeonians expand

After the departure of the Mycenaeans from south-eastern Anatolia, the Paeonians who had stayed behind in various centres were in a minority. In time their kith and kin must have joined them, which is confirmed by Suhis first of Carchemish in his inscription Carchemish A1a. Other voluntary small scale migrations history will not have recorded. But the truth of this assertion is fundamental and very credible. Because, in mixed societies, sooner rather than later, bilingualism starts, leading to the domination of one language, which is usually the language spoken by the majority. As already mentioned, the Paeonians were in minority after the departure of the Mycenaeans, but their language prevailed, which could only have happened if waves of new immigrants were continuously arriving in the country and revitalizing the language and the culture of their predecessors. This same process we will see again after the Armenians' entry into Urartu, but in that case we will have attestations from various writers and evidence from the land where the new waves settled.

The conditions in south-eastern Anatolia must have stabilized within a generation or two, enabling the majority population, the Hurrians, to establish rulerships in a few centres, such as Melid and Carchemish. This may be inferred from the names of the kings up to the beginning of the first millennium BC, which, also confirms that the Hurrian nobility had survived the destructions of the early 12th century BC.

Historians of language, as a whole, disagree with my claim, and assert that it was the Luwians who took the country over, establishing kingdoms and left various inscriptions in hieroglyphic script, but they do not tell us where the Hurrian population disappeared to. Furthermore, they claim that the Luwian language speakers were driven in front of the newcomers, the force that destroyed Khattusha and other cities, but never mention where these newcomers, also, disappeared to; they completely ignore and fail to account for them in their elaborations. However, there is evidence that the Hurrians, at least in Carchemish, were armenicised before the 6th century BC. These people who were in majority before the 10th century, due to the waves of Paeonian migrations into their lands, had become a minority, and, by early 6th century BC, when the proto-Armenians entered Urartu they, too, were a party to the adventure and settled on the northern coastline of Lake Van, becoming known as the "Khorkhorunik'" (Khor in Armenian means Hurrian). The proto-Armenian Yarairaisa of Carchemish in his inscription A 6.3, names one of the languages he was fully versed in as "Sura", which transcribes as 'Hura' (= Hurrian). Linguists on the whole claim that the language of the hieroglyphic inscriptions was Luwian (except Barnett) and they explain their views in scholarly fashion, which makes the theory rather persuasive; but to a discerning reader the contradictions inherent in such theories outweigh their usefulness. They do not perhaps realise that it is they who are slowly and carefully creating a new language, which one kind linguist told me was a younger version of Luwian (Lycian?), a characterisation with which I agree. It *is* a younger version, in fact so young that it is the product of the last 40 years.

The excavations at Boğazköy, the centre of Hittite government, yielded thousands of inscribed tablets. Of these 99 per cent were in the Hittite cuneiform, and the remaining 1 per cent were Palaite, Luwian and Hurrian. Considering the scarcity of hieroglyphic texts Barnett asks "is it not extraordinary that they (the hieroglyphics) should be so scarce in the Hittite native home and most abundant only in their most newly acquired provinces?"[100] It is Barnett, again, who says: "The language of the hieroglyphic inscriptions is neither Luwian, Palaite, nor the language of the Hittite cuneiform. It does not tally with Lycian, Lydian (these last two are accepted as a younger version of the Luwian) or Phrygian, but appears to belong to the *satem* group."[101]

The hieroglyphic script is mainly syllabic with a few

alphabetic signs and many logograms, which act as words or determinatives. The syllabic and alphabetic signs, at least, conform to an acrophonic principle. Every language can have its own acrophonia if need be. Linguists do not tell us anything about this subject (except Barnett), which is the easiest to demonstrate and has the power to establish which language the hieroglyphic signs belong to.

It may be true, and is expected that some Hittites were driven out by the Sea People's movement. Most of these ended up in Palestine, which can be verified from the Bible. The few that had stayed in south-eastern Anatolia could not revive their culture nor could these few be, even by a miracle, the only Luwian speakers. Therefore, the claim that these inscriptions were in the Luwian language is untenable. Beside, "there is an absence of evidence that Luwian survived into the Iron Age."[102]

Archaeological excavations, particularly those in Melid and Carchemish unearthed various artefacts of Hittite provenance. But, these finds were those that the newcomers had brought with them. They had ransacked, looted and destroyed Khattusha and other Hittite cities on their way, which means they had robbed the original owners, the Hittites, of these artefacts. It seems probable that in extensive excavations in the Sasoon district, where the Urumeans and the Kaska had settled, and around the confluence of the Euphrates and Arsanias rivers where the Mushki had settled, artefacts of such nature would come to light. It is not the findings of the excavations that are being challenged but the interpretation of the circumstances of their presence.

One last point in this connection remains. It is known that after the 7th century BC the hieroglyphic inscriptions in south-eastern Anatolia ceased. Why did this happen, and where the people responsible for the inscriptions disappear to? We only know of the proto-Armenians, who around this time left south-eastern Anatolia and entered Urartu. Is it not extraordinary that linguists know all the shortcomings of their theories, and chose to ignore them? If they were to take history seriously and face the anomalies of their theory, they would have to admit that the language of the hieroglyphic inscriptions matches only one nations' language, that is the Armenians, the speakers of which were in south-eastern Anatolia, or in the country of Aram, from the 12th to the beginning of the 6th centuries BC, and, it was this Aram habitation that earned them the appellation Armenian, which only means 'People of Aram'.

To reinforce further the Aram habitation of the Armenians, prior entering Urartu, we have the proto-Georgians, the northern neighbours of the proto-Armenians, who called them Somekhi (not Armenian). Somekhi means 'inhabitant of Suhmu' (the ancient Hittite Zuhmu). Suhmu comprised the north-eastern parts of Aram and included the kingdom of Melid Kummanu. The Georgians for the past, at least, 2,600 years have been the northern neighbours of the Armenians; but it must have been in the north-eastern parts of Aram that they had for the first time been in contact with them, hence the appellation Somekhi.

CHAPTER 3

THE PAEONIAN MIGRATIONS INTO ANATOLIA

Voluntary and forced migrations

Starting with the second half of the 13th century BC, the Paeonians began to migrate to Anatolia in waves. The voluntary migrations of smaller numbers are not recorded by history; but a few of the forced ones or the migrations of large populations are mentioned in the works of some ancient and more recent writers. Below I list eight such waves coming into Anatolia and discuss each in turn:

1. The Paeonians of the Trojan War and its aftermath
2. The Pelagonian Paeonians' migration to Anatolia with the Phrygians at the end of the 9th century BC.[103]
3. The Scythian and Cimmerian pressure in 8th to 7th centuries forced some Paeonians to leave their country for Anatolia.[104]
4. Darius I in 510 BC instructed Megabazos to deport the Paeonians east of Lake Prasias to Anatolia.[105]
5. The disappearance of the Paeonians east of the River Strymon due to pressure from the Macedonians to the west and from the Thracians to the east.[106]
6. Alexander the Great's expedition to Asia included Paeonian cavalry[107] and Agrianian infantry.[108]

7. The Paeonian people carried along with the Celts (Galataeans) to Anatolia around 275 BC.[109]
8. At the beginning of 2nd century BC, the Paeonians disappeared from the Balkans.[110]

1. The Paeonians of the Trojan War and its aftermath

This subject has already been discussed in the previous chapters.

2. The Pelagonian Paeonians' migration to Anatolia with the Phrygians

In the Balkans the Phrygians, according to Herodotus (7.73), were known as the 'Brygi' or the Brygians. By the 9th century BC the prosperity of these people had reached its zenith. At the end of the same century the Phrygians moved to Anatolia as a strong and cohesive nation, and established a mighty kingdom where there had previously been the Hittites.[111] The Pelagonian/ Paeonians, too, had joined their neighbours, the Brygians, in this fateful exodus.[112] The Assyrians called the newly-arrived Phrygians 'Mushki', taking the original name of the eastern Mushki, which had already collapsed, and most probably, the various tribes had dispersed to the various parts of Anatolia.

The Pelagonian Paeonians, as in the Balkans, kept their neighbourly connections with the Phrygians and settled to the east of them in Tabal (later Cappadocia). This is inferred from various names and events of late 9th and early 8th centuries, which are:

a) With the collapse of the eastern Mushki, the Pelagonian Paeonians had withdrawn to the lands of the northern Taurus mountains, which was known as Tabal. Here they had established a small kingdom under Tuatte and his son Kikki, which is testified by the inscriptions of Shalmaneser III of Assyria. By the beginning of the 8th century BC this kingdom must have received a sudden stimulus, because the next two kings, Tuwatis and Wasusaramimasa, started to use the style of 'great king', which could have only have happened if a mass of new immigrants of the same language and culture had arrived in the country. The move to the northern lands of the Taurus had also enabled them to be near to the other Paeonians of Gurgum and Carchemish, who had already established or usurped kingdoms starting with the 10th century BC.

b) The name of the old king Tuatte's son, Kikki, derives from the Assyrian inscriptions, therefore, it is the Assyrian rendering, which, as usual, adds a 'ki' ending to the name. The stem is 'Kik', which transcribes as 'Sis' — we find this stem in the city name of Sissu, which is the same as the later Sis, the name of the capital city of the Armenian kingdom of Cilicia of 11th to 14th centuries AD. When the proto-Armenians moved into Urartu, c. 588/87 BC, the people of Tabal settled to the east of the highlands under the name of Sis as Sisakeans and the country became known as Sisakan.

c) To the west of Pelagonia, in the Balkans, there was a lake on a high altitude, which they had named 'Lychnidus' (the present-day Lake Ohrid). The lands of Sisakan, in eastern Armenia, also contained the southern half of present-day Lake Sevan which, being on a high altitude, had an extraordinary resemblance to the Lake Lychnidus the Pelagonian proto-Armenians had left behind. Therefore, the obvious thing to do was to name this new lake after the one they had known in the Balkans as Lychnidus.

3. Due to Scythian and Cimmerian pressure in the 8th to 7th centuries many Paeonians left for Anatolia

There is no evidence to indicate where this third wave of Paeonians settled in Anatolia. It may well be that most of them ended up in Cilicia Tracheia and north of it in Tabal districts, because this migration coincides with the period when minor kingdoms in these parts of Anatolia start to emerge.

The only Assyrian information about a Hay/Paeonian presence in south-eastern Anatolia comes from the inscription of Tiglath-Pileser III (745-727 BC), who mentions them but does not tell us where had they settled. However, this testimony confirms that Hays and Paeonians were the same people, in addition to validating the claim that they were in Anatolia. The inscription on the Nimrut Tablet (rev.) section 799 of 728 BC refers to various tribute bearers while Tiglath-Pileser was in northern Syria, and reads: "The Mas'ai, Temai, Sab'ai, *Haiapai*, Badanai . . . on the border of the lands of the setting sun, whom no one knew, and whose home is afar off . . ."[113] Of course the compound name of Haiapai means 'Hay Paeonians'.

The Paeonian migrations into Anatolia, listed as numbers 4 to 8, belong to the period when the proto-Armenians had already entered and settled in various districts of Urartu, as we shall see later. Therefore, these items are not, strictly speaking, a part of this study. Since no other individual scholar or scholarly work appears to have ever researched, discussed, or even noticed the topic, I think, it might be useful to enumerate the various localities where the subjects of this enquiry had settled. This will also reinforce my claim that the Hays were a Balkan nation, where they were known as Paeonians.

4. Darius I had the Paeonians living
east of Lake Prasias deported to Anatolia

According to Herodotus (5.17 and 5.98) some of these Paeonians escaped back to their homelands with the help of the islanders of the Aegean. The number of the escapees, under the noses of the Persians, could not have been great. Herodotus also tells us that the tribes of the Paeonians deported by Megabazos, Darius's commander, were the Siriopaeonians, the Paioplai and all the others as far as Lake Prasias. The settlement area of this large wave of Paeonian immigrants was Cappadocia, bordering Phrygia to the west and Armenia to the east, which lands had already been vacated by the movement of the Tabalian proto-Armenians into the eastern districts (Sisakan) of Armenia. The time of their arrival was about 75 years after the proto-Armenians had moved into Urartu. It must have been soon after the arrival of these people that the name Siriopaeonian, in Cappadocia, was changed or shortened by other nations to Sirian, and "in order to distinguish them from the true Syrians with tanned complexion, the Greeks called them 'White Syrians'" (Strabo 12.3.9).

The later kingdoms and kings of Cappadocia, until the time it became a Roman province, were all Syrio-Paeonians, therefore, by origin, Hays/Armenians.

5. Macedonian pressure in the west and Thracian tribes to the east forced the Paeonians east of the River Strymon to migrate to Anatolia

This concerns the people of Odomantis, about whom Herodotus (5.15) says that they were Paeonians. In this particular instance the Odomantians are not named, but the geographical location mentioned can only apply to them, because the Paeoplai and the Siriopaeonians had already left the Balkans for Anatolia and the Doberes had moved west to the valleys of the River Axius.[114]

Close to the end of 5th century BC the people of Odomantis, which was to the north of Edonis and the Pangaeon mountains, left their homelands and migrated directly to Armenia under pressure, particularly, from the Thracian tribes. Their settlement area in the highlands was between Sophene, Acilisene and Asthianene extending to the eastern banks of the Euphrates. Their new habitation they named Odomantis after their original homelands in the Balkans. In the early 2nd century BC this district was under the rule of Zareh, also known as the *stratekos* (general) Zariadres.[115]

It was at about this time that the Paeonians of Bottiaea, but particularly those of the city of Gordynia in central Paeonia, on the western banks of the upper Axius river, left in large numbers for Anatolia under pressure from the Macedonians. These immigrants settled in southern Armenia between today's rivers Tigris, Habur Çay and Bohtan Çay (Kentrites). Their new habitation was a mountainous country referred to by Xenophon as the land of the Carduchi (Kurds). After their arrival, which was before Alexander the Great's passage through the country, the mountains were renamed Gordaean (Korduatz) and the lands Gordyene (the Armenian Korduk' which in the past used to be written as Gorduk').[116] Xenophon in his *Anabasis* passed through these lands, which he describes as Carduchi country. Obviously, the people of Gordynia had not yet arrived; otherwise, Xenophon would have recognized and mentioned them.

6. Alexander the Great's army had Paeonian cavalry and Agrianian infantry

It is well documented that Alexander's army had a Paeonian cavalry under the command of Ariston[117] and a large number of Agrianian infantry.[118] After the battle of Gaugamela these mercenaries disappeared and were not mentioned again.

Merker[119] is of the opinion that they might have been allowed to go home, meaning Paeonia. I find this most unlikely, considering that their compatriots had already established themselves in nearby Gordyene. These fighting men must have known of the migrations of their people into Anatolia since the 12th century BC, which must also have been reflected in the diminishing population of Paeonia. Also, while passing through Gordyene, they must have met some of their compatriots. Therefore, it is hard to imagine that they would travel all the way to Paeonia to return to Armenia soon after. I think these fighting men must have joined their brethren in Gordyene, in southern Armenia.

7. The Paeonians were carried along when the Celts invaded Anatolia

According to an epigram from the city of Tlos in Lycia, which Stephanus Byzantinus had preserved,[120] the Paeonians moved into Anatolia along with the Celts (Galataeans) in the course of their invasion of Asia Minor (c. 275 BC). This wave of Paeonian immigrants settled in and around Nisibis (Mtsbin), which became known as Mygdonia, after their previous Balkan homelands. Strabo (Frag. 7.36) says that these Mygdonians, beside settling in Nisibis, also, spread from the ancient Zegma (Bridge) at Tapsacus (the middle Syrian Euphrates) to the new Zegma in Commagene and further north to the Masis mountains.

8. At the beginning of the 2nd century the Paeonians disappear from the Balkans

This is the final stage of the Paeonian migrations. Kreischmer and Krahe[121] say that some of the Paeonians moved south to the Peloponnese, but most migrated to Anatolia.[122] Of course, this does not mean that everyone moved away; there will always be people who will not part from their possessions or friends. What it means is that Paeonia, as a viable country with mostly Paeonian population, ceased to exist and became part of Macedonia under the hegemony of the Romans, who divided it into several districts.

The last king of Paeonia, Dropion, had disappeared from the historical records under unknown circumstances. It may well be that the start of these last migrations had a direct influence on the dissolution of the kingdom, the reason being that the Paeonians of this last migration were those from the capital city Bylazora and from Amphaxitis (both sides of the River Axius). It is almost certain that these people settled to the west of the Ararat mountains, as it is there, in a depression surrounded by high mountains, that they established the new city of Bylazora, which is known to us as Bayazed in Armenian.

PART
II

CHAPTER 4

THE KINGDOM OF CARCHEMISH

After the settlement of the Paeonians, in various districts of south-eastern Anatolia (country of Aram), a new culture and language appeared on the scene of this essentially Hurrian country by the 10th century BC. This part will examine the achievements of these new people, who from now on will be called the proto-Armenians.

Carchemish

The history of the proto-Armenians of Karakamis starts very early in the 10th century BC, when Suhis I married princess Watis, the daughter of the last Hurrian king Ura Tark ('the great thunder'). The proto-Armenian rule of Karakamis, starting with Suhis I, comprises eight kings, of which the first four represent a dynasty, but there is no certainty that the remainder belonged also to the same line. It is known that the last three kings belonged to a continuous line, that of Astiruwa, but how were these connected, if they were, to the first dynasty of Suhis remains uncertain.

Ruler	Date	Source of Attestation
Suhis I	c.970?	A 1a; A 1b; A 4b
Asatuwatimaza	c.950?	A 11a; A 11b; A 27u
Suhis II	c.925?	A 14a; A 14b; A 2; A 11a; A 11b

The proto-Armenian kingdoms of Aram
R. Halys
Karaburna
Bogca
L. Tatta
Caesa
(Maz
Shinukhtu?
T U W A N A
Bor
Tuwana
Khubishna
Atuna
R. Sar
Si
CILICIA CAM
CILICIA
Hilakku
R. Cydnus
R.
Calycadnus
CILICIA ASPERA
Illubru
Adana
Tarsus
P I R I N D U
R.
Lamus
QUE (K
Ura
(Olba)

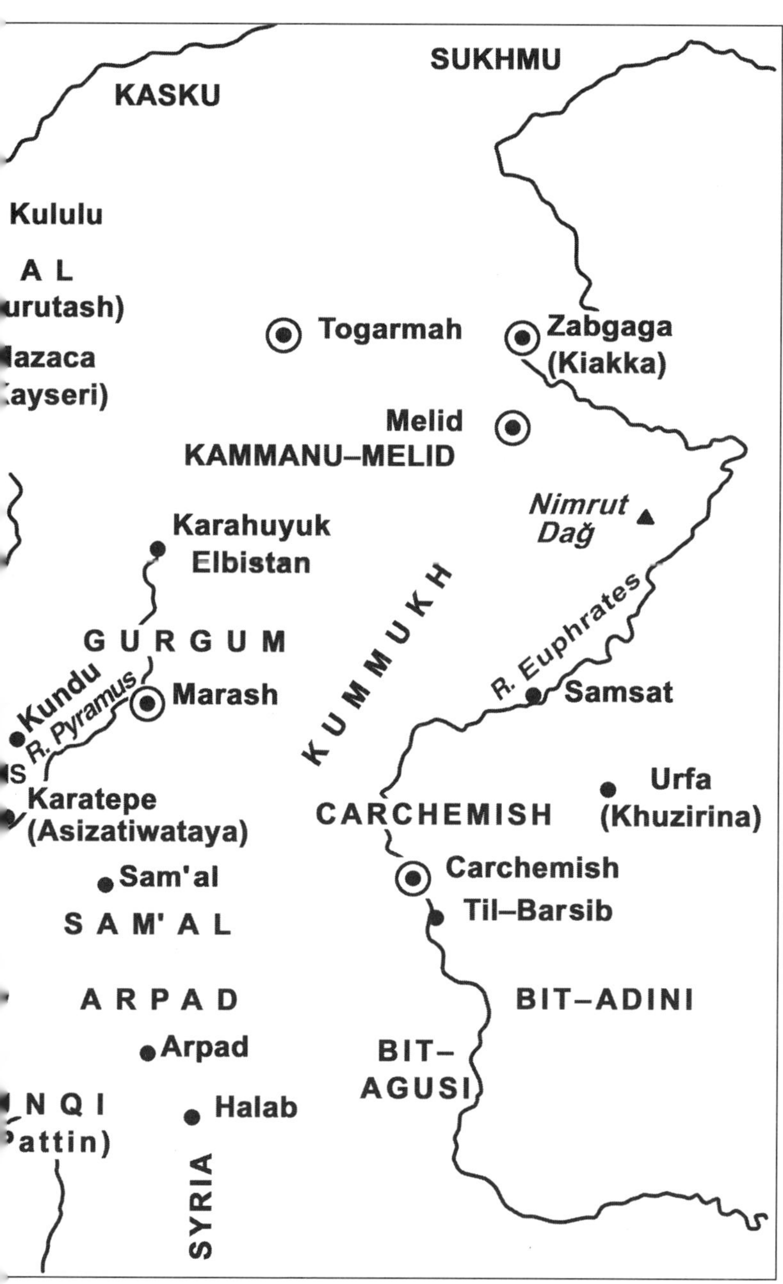
KASKU
SUKHMU
Kululu
A L
urutash)
azaca
ayseri)
Togarmah
Zabgaga
(Kiakka)
Melid
KAMMANU–MELID
Nimrut Dağ
Karahuyuk
Elbistan
GURGUM
KUMMUKH
Kundu
R. Pyramus
R. Euphrates
Marash
Samsat
S
Urfa
(Khuzirina)
Karatepe
(Asizatiwataya)
CARCHEMISH
Sam'al
Carchemish
SAM'AL
Til–Barsib
ARPAD
BIT–ADINI
Arpad
BIT–
AGUSI
NQI
attin)
Halab
SYRIA

Katuwa	c.900?	A 2; A 3; A 11a-c; A 12; A 13d; A 23
Sangara	c.878-848	Ashurnasirpal II; Shalmaneser III
Astiruwa	c.785?	A 15b; A 20b.1; A 27.1; A 27mm; Körkün A2
Kamana	770?-738	Cekke; A 4a; A 17b; A 22b; A 32; A 6-7; A 15b
Pisiris	738-717	Tiglath-Pileser III; Sargon III

In addition to the eight names of kings, there are also two most important ones, who had exercised power either as regent or prime minister. These two were father and son, who were not related to the ruling house.

Yarairaisa	780?-754	A 6; A 7; A 15b; A 24.4
Sastura	754-724?	Cekke; A 20b.8; A 22b

Suhis I

The name means 'hope', which in Classical Armenian is written as Yoys (pronounced 'Huys'), but its archaic form was Yoyis ('Huyis'). This is, perhaps, the most difficult name to explain, because it does not adhere to the normal transcription rules, which must have been the reason why the recomposed name-lists of Khorenatsi's prehistory do not mention it as one of the old Armenian kings. In fact, it is the only name, which was also that of his grandson, that is missing; and yet Suhis's son, the ruler between the two Suhises, Asatuwatimaza, is recorded as Amasia (see the next name). In view of these difficulties, I feel a lengthy explanation is in order, because Suhis was the first proto-Armenian ruler of Karakamis (from now on Carchemish).

The hieroglyphic script had a 'ya' syllable in the form of 'ia' (sign 210), but not 'y', 'yi' and 'yu'. The scribe, in order to write this name, had to use a syllabic sign which was phonetically the nearest to 'yu' (pronounced 'hu'). This takes care of the first syllable 'Su' of Suhis in the following manner: 'Su' > 'Hu', normal transcription; 'Hu' > 'Yu' phonetically identical. The second syllable of the name, 'his' developing to 'yis' creates bigger problems, because in this case the 'yis' part of 'Yuyis' is pronounced exactly as it is written, and in the Classical Armenian language an 'H' > 'Y' phonetic development is not attested (the 'hing' to 'yisun', 'hadanel' to 'yodel' and 'het' to 'yet' changes do not interfere with the phonetics of the words as in all cases the initial 'y' is pronounced as 'h'), though we do not know exactly how the proto-Armenians pronounced this name. There is another anomaly very much like this one, which may serve as mitigating evidence that such minor deviations should be expected from a script of limited scope, such as the case of 'Z' phoneme used in place of 'Y', which did not exist in the script (see below).

We know nothing about Suhis (I) except what he tells us in his two inscriptions, Carchemish A4b and A1a, both of which are damaged. Apparently Suhis had not usurped power. He tells us that the Great Thunder (Ura Tark), the last Hurrian king of Carchemish, had entrusted him with the throne of the country, which makes sense in view of the fact that he had married the king's daughter Watis, who must have been the eldest of the children, because her inscription (A1b) exhibits a certain authority in the statement of "Esteem my great brave husband; honours for my person are by the same token honours for him." However, the inscription informs us that the covetous son (his brother-in-law, whose name has partly survived) of the deceased king Great Thunder wanted the throne for himself. The ensuing battle for power was the start of the troubles between the proto-Armenians and the Hurrian population.

Suhis's inscription (A 1a), or what is left of it, starts with his exploits and the enlargement of the borders of the kingdom. It is a balanced account of affairs because he also tells us of his failure; such as his failure to breach the city walls of Saparaga wherein his enemy, a certain Hazanamasa (perhaps this should be read as 'Haya-na-masa' = 'belonging to the Hay people') had shut himself up, which means that Hazanamasa had taken over one of Suhis's cities and would not surrender or leave it.

Next, Suhis tells us of his philanthropy, which is most interesting, particularly, in the case of the Hays (proto-Armenians). He says: "The Hay people of the city I pacified by force, and supplied with provisions in order to lessen their destitution."[1] I think this refers to new waves of Paeonians who had arrived hungry and destitute; it is remarkable that he does not call them Paeonians, but Hay people.

The designation Hay is written as 'Ha-za-u-na-na', which Hawkins transliterates as 'Haiu-nana'.[2] One has to agree with this transliteration, because nowhere else in the inscriptions I have studied, does the 'u' of the Hazau follow the 'za' syllable and the whole phrase is qualified with the affinity-indicating word of 'nana'; other inscriptions, including that of Azatiwata, have used the word 'nana', but with a different spelling (see Karatepe Text sentences V, XXV, XXX, and XXXII wherein the word is the proto-Armenian 'naχ-na' which has the meanings 'in the first place', 'before', and 'originally' — the 'nana' of sentence LX is a completely different word and means 'nullify').

Suhis continues to narrate his experiences of the new arrivals and it seems the main trouble-makers were the priests belonging to these migrants. He says that his wife was at his side when these migrant priests were brought to his presence, and he enlisted them to the service of the god Tark. According to Suhis, his son, too, was involved in the pacification of the destitute by distributing goods and provisions from the crown stores. An image of Suhis was erected for which he solicits annual sacrifice of a lamb and the offer of bread.

The inscription ends with a repeated curse on Hazanama, and begs the god Tark to move him out from the city of Saparaga. There is a curious point in this last mention of the name of his adversary. It is written as 'Hazamana', which at first sight one might think is a mistake. It is no mistake, but a play on words. The 'mana' ending of the name means 'to take a walk', which has replaced the 'nama' ending for emphasis, and, perhaps wishful thinking; there are similar examples in the inscriptions.

Asatuwatimaza

The sense of this name is 'Preacher of Amity', which derives from 'asa' ('says, preaches, tells') + 'tu-wa' ('give-come' = 'be, become') + 'ti' ('body, group, as a whole') + 'maza' ('paste together, adjoin, coalesce' — 'maz' transcribes as 'matz' from which the modern word 'matzown/yoghurt' derives). The Classical Armenian recomposition of this name was 'Amasia' ('am' = 'together, adjoined' + 'as' = 'say, preach, tell' — the same as the 'asa' initial stem of the old name), which has the identical sense of 'preacher of amity'. Scholars transcribe the ancient name as 'Astuwatamanza', which is a corruption of the original written name, and renders translation practically impossible.

Asatuwatimaza has left a badly damaged short inscription (A14b) commemorating the erection of a gate. Otherwise, there is not much information about this 10th century king of Carchemish, except what appears in the inscriptions of Suhis II, his son, and Katuwa, his grandson. In the case of the first four names, the dynasty of Suhis I, there are no outside independent sources to attest them or even indirectly give us some information.

Suhis I, the father of Asatuwatimaza, in his inscription A 1a mentions the birth name of his son as "Halpa-BIRD-pina", which means 'devoted to the praise of Kupapa'. Therefore, the Asatuwatimaza must have been his demotic name, from which it can be inferred that there was much Hurrian unrest in Carchemish because of the loss of the rulership to the proto-Armenians. The same unrests are also referred to by Suhis II, his son, and graphically described by Katuwa, his grandson.

Suhis II

He was the grandson of Suhis I and bears the same name. What I have seen of his inscriptions they are all fragmented and difficult to make full sense of. There are parts, which can be read as sentences, but isolated sentences do not give the full story. Such a sentence, both legible and interesting, highlights his claim of being a proto-Armenian. It reads: "wa-mu-a a-ma za ta-ti-ia za (BAR) sa-la Ha-za pi-ia za-a", which means "I was raised to the throne and joined the noble status of Hay fathers", and adds "ti-pa ara ma-ha wa mu TAPARA za na" = "god took his soul, I pay homage to him" (A 14a, lines 2-3).

In this extract Suhis confirms that the rulership was in the hands of the proto-Armenians (Hays) and that he himself was a proto-Armenian. Katuwa, Suhis's son, confirms that there were instances of unrest in the time of his father, which means that the Hurrian population and the descendants of the last Hurrian king Ura Tark were still trying to take possession of the throne.

Katuwa

The name means 'solid person'. The 'kat' > 'kay' means 'solid, firm', 'there is, exists' and the 'uwa' > 'oga' (genitive) 'a person, soul, being', except that 'uwa' was a titular ending used only in the names of kings, such as Astir*uwa*. The recomposed Classical Armenian name of this king, in Book 1.19 of Khorenatsi is Kaypak, of which the 'kay' stem is the same as the 'kat' of Katuwa, but the second stem of the name, 'pak', is not found in proto-Armenian; it means 'fearsome, stupefying, dread', which gives the name the meaning of 'fearsomely solid/firm'. Katuwa had a long reign and was a prolific producer of inscriptions, which are historically invaluable, even though he does not appear to be attested by the Assyrians, as at his time Assyria had not yet acquired the might, which became evident during the reign of Sangara and after. In inscription A 2 he tells us of his succession and joy in joining "the status of ruling Hay forefathers". He describes the happy games people used to play, and the condition of participating in such games being the gift of a lamb to be taken to the temple of the god Tark. But half way through line 4, the mood suddenly changes; good times are over and hard times begin.

The A 3 inscription has at least two lines at the beginning missing. What we have starts with: "Chosen person of Carchemish, city of the great god Tark and the kingdom was happy. But, because of my inheritance, the god-given kingdom of my forefathers, troubles started. A certain Urhi Sarma, a descendant of Ura Tark, attacked and looted the city, but thanks to the gods' intervention the atrocities stopped" — and, as he puts it, "the action of the enemy achieved nothing and my kingdom was restored" (actually, the word he uses is 'resurrected' — 'yaru', which has also the meanings of 'reanimated, stood-up').

As in A 2 inscription, A 11a also records the line "the great kingdom's crown of noble Hay fathers came to me." And adds: "this was the reason for the disturbances that befell me, which had spread to the whole country and were double of those of my father's time. The alternative was for me not to become the ruler." In line 5 he repeats that the kingdom was looted and adds: "The enemy selected with great care and reverence ten reliquaries of the dead, taking them to his own palace together with the kingdom's throne as booty."

Inscription A 11b is about the arrival in the city of a certain Nanuwa (a Hurrian name), a descendant of Ura Tark, the last Hurrian king of Carchemish. Nanuwa had studied rhetoric in the city of Kawaza and knew how to conduct a debate. Katuwa says that "everybody admired him" and that he, for his part, gave him advancement by entrusting him with the governorship of the city of Muzikia. Unfortunately, he was badly let down by Nanuwa's devious plans and had to get rid of him.

The opening lines of inscription A 11c are again missing.

The subject here is presented as a devil worshipper whom he wishes to become "blind, and as a vagabond, to go in circles in foreign countries and never again find his own country." The continuation of this curse is something I have never come across in any other inscription. It shows how wretched he felt and how difficult his rulership had become. He asks the god Tark to "destroy his (enemy's) males' innate ability to give pleasure to their women, by means of their natural glory, their members for entering in order to become fathers. His women possessed by evil spirits to copulate with their fathers. This person set my city on fire, he was a descendant of Ura Tark."

In the inscription A 11a.2, it is worth noticing what the clever scribe who executed it had done. He must have noticed the anomaly of using sign 377, the 'za' syllable, to express the 'ya' phonetic in the name of 'Haya'. He has made a minor change in the appearance of this sign, as if to make it known that this new sign 377, stands for the 'ya' syllable. Unfortunately, we do not see this rearranged sign 377 in later inscriptions.

Katuwa has also left a badly damaged inscription (A23) of his matured age, executed on the occasion of the death of his wife Ana. This inscription has great cultural value, as it outlines the custom of how the corpse of the departed was treated.

Sangara

This name has the sense of 'shepherd of his flock'. The 'san' of Sangara means to nurture and care for an adopted son. 'Gara' (the genitive form) is the same as the present Armenian 'garn' meaning 'lamb'; therefore, a 'caretaker of his adopted lambs'. This name is still popular in its shortened version of Garnik and that is how it appears in Khorenatsi's prehistory.

It is a mystery why no inscriptions of this king have been found. Obviously, he must have been a very popular ruler in order to earn such a demotic name for himself. Due to the want of information it is not known whether he had any connections with the House of Katuwa or whether he was a usurper who enjoyed a long reign in the course of which he was much respected and liked. The part of the name, which has the sense of 'adopted' is perhaps a clue to his succession, and could be a cryptic marker to tell of his usurpation of the throne.

The campaigns of Ashurnasirpal II (883-859 BC) between the years 882 and 867 mention Sangara[3] couple of times as king of Carchemish, who presented valuable tribute and auxiliaries without resistance. After the accession of Shalmaneser III (858-824 BC) in Assyria, the northern Syrian city states of Sam'al, Bit-Adini and Unqi initiated an alliance against him; Sangara, too, was a party to this alliance of 858 BC.[4] Unfortunately, Shalmaneser prevailed, the alliance disintegrated and some participants were punished. It appears Sangara was forgiven for his transgression, perhaps due to the heavy tribute imposed on Carchemish. Starting with Ashurnasirpal II, in 882, Sangara is a regular tribute payer, which serves as confirmation of his rule in Carchemish for the years 882 to 848 BC. It is not known when Sangara died or at what date his rule came to an end.

Astiruwa

The name means either 'mighty thinker' or 'mighty truth-teller' ('ast' = 'might, influence, inform' + 'ir' = 'truth, think, a thing' + 'uwa' = 'person, soul, being' in the genitive — 'uwa' is a titular ending for rulership). Our knowledge of Astiruwa's rule derives from the inscriptions of Yarairaisa and Ilapikasa of Körkün. Kamana, his son, has also written about him, but the inscriptions involved are all fragmented and impossible to make sense of, except for noticing the name 'Astiru' in a few places.

Astiruwa is remembered by Khorenatsi (book 1.12) as Erast, which is an anagram of 'Ast-ir' ('Ir-ast', but the 'i' in time became 'e'). He is also known as Ara the Fair, which is due to the fact that the later Armenian account of Astiru has been mythologized and made into a romance. But there are certain aspects of the story that are in concordance with what Yarairaisa and Ilapikasa of Körkün write. Astiruwa died young, which is confirmed by the young family illustrated in A6 and A7 inscriptions and made explicit in the Körkün inscription of Ilapikasa (lines 1-2: 'hati sa na manu ha' = 'he died while young'). His death was due to the plague, which devastated Carchemish around 775 BC. It appears this was the same plague that spread to Tabal where the king, Tuwatis (Aramayis), also became infected and died (see Kululu I.1b inscription). His wife's name was Tuwarasaisa, meaning 'the king took this one for himself (as wife)', which reflects a certain demotic resentment. Perhaps, the king could have done better, but most probably Tuwarasaisa was a foreign bride, which is reflected in her recomposed Classical Armenian name of Nuard, meaning 'elegant/comely bride'.

According to the later story, Astiruwa died in a battle when his son was 12 years old, but the Armenian source names this son as Arayan Ara (Yarairaisa), which is confusing due to the fact that the story had been gleaned from the 'songs' and poems of later bards and minstrels. Nevertheless, there is some truth in the story, which is confirmed by Yarairaisa in his inscriptions A6 and A7, wherein he says that the son was Kamana (Hawanak) who "was an immature boy".

The story also tells us that the river name Araxi, in Armenia, was changed to Eraskh, in remembrance of Erast (Astir), which does not make sense to us, because the name Araxi consists from the Armenian prefix 'ar' plus the Greek word 'axi' ('ar' = 'first, primary' + 'axi' is the Greek stem meaning 'worth', therefore 'araxi' = 'foremost worthy/value'), which derives from the river name of Axius (the Worthy) in Paeonia. Eraskh is the translation of Araxi into pure Armenian, wherein 'era' is equivalent to 'ar', in other words has the same meaning, and 'sχ' is the stem of the word 'sχrali', giving us the meaning 'foremost worthy/value/wonder'. Nevertheless, there is a very good archaic reason why such a story was created which we shall see in the next part (Chpater 15) as the proto-Armenians move to Urartu.

There is a chronological problem concerning the demise of Sangara and the accession of Astiruwa. This involves a gap of 30 to 50 years between these two rulers. The only source that throws light on the matter is that of the Körkün inscription of Ilapikasa, who was a cousin, once removed, of Astiruwa. Ilapikasa says: "At the time my father ruled, he had provided Astiruwa with soldiers of the state for his struggle", and adds that "after growing strong he prevailed and became ruler of that great region. He became mighty. He begot many offspring and became a father." The Körkün inscription confirms that after the demise of Sangara, anarchy prevailed in Carchemish, and much later the great-grandson of either Sangara or his firstborn Astiruwa was fighting for his hereditary right to succeed to the throne of the city-state.

Yarairaisa

The name means 'attached to the thinker/truthful'. Scholarship has shortened this name to Yariris, which makes no sense grammatically; Yarira would have been better. In any case, the inscriptions spell the name as I have done. His Classical Armenian name was Arayan Ara which, again, does not make sense, because the name Ara cannot be explained in the Armenian language. I believe the original recomposition of the name must have been Erayan Erah which, in time, due to reasons I do not know, changed to Arayan Ara; Erayan Erah means the 'most honourable'. The Armenian traditions also call him Kardos, which is truly remarkable, because Kardos means 'erudite'.

The inscriptions of Yarairaisa are very important, because they are the sole sources which shed light on proto-Armenian life in Carchemish and on Astiruwa and his family in the first half of 8th century BC.

Yarairaisa tells us of the circumstances, which forced him to take control of the kingdom. The king, Astiruwa (Erast) had died in the plague of c. 775 BC, leaving behind his young family and the kingdom to his care. It appears Yarairaisa thought a lot of Astiruwa, as on more than one occasion he calls him "that great person".

He also tells us that he was fully versed in many languages, which he lists as Hurrian (Sura), Mysian (Musa), Phrygian (Musaka), Assyrian (Asura) and Mannaean (Mana); if we add to these his own language, proto-Armenian, and for him the most important language of Aramaean, the number grows to seven languages. It is possible that he also knew Urartian and Greek. He says his "father had told him that knowledge of many languages brings success", and that "when they were young his father had tutored him and his brothers". The thirst for languages, in his youth, had driven him to "travel in all the countries" mentioned, in order to learn their languages, as if "he had no other care in the world".

The inscriptions A 6 and A 7 were executed soon after the death of the king, Astiruwa, and the coronation of Kamana, which can be dated to c. 770 BC. Inscription A 15b, was executed, as he tells us, ten years after the plague when Kamana and his brothers had grown to become young men and he himself was well matured.

Inscription A 6 describes Kamana as an immature young boy on the throne and how after the coronation 30 to 40 invited guests stood up and continuously applauded him.

He describes how young Kamana, dressed up as a great king, enters the court in order to pass judgement on various criminals: "He took the sword (symbol of adjudication) and sat on the throne. An offender was brought in who was burdened with many cares and tormented by anguish, asking for forgiveness. He was granted a pardon by the young king."

In the same inscription, in lines 6-7 Yarairaisa prays for the well-being of the young king Kamana, and says: "Great charger god Tark, great god Sun and god Kupapa let him not come to difficulties, always protect and grant him grandeur."

According to inscription A24 of Kamana, Yarairaisa died in 754 BC in Assyria, where he had travelled, "with the gift of a hundred horses", to be present at the coronation of the new king, Ashur-nirari V (754-745 BC). He was taken ill and in great pain passed away. The inscription also adds that the whole of the kingdom was set in mourning and there was much confused talk about the passing away of the 'learned one'. The Assyrian king had him enshrouded by his servants and made the funeral oration. This part of the inscription confirms the Armenian tradition that Arayan Ara died in a foreign country.

Kamana

The name means 'devoid of will and say', that is, this king had no say in matters concerning the running of the state. His recomposed Classical Armenian name (Khorenatsi, Book 1.19) was Hawanak, which means a 'consenter', which is in full concordance with the proto-Armenian name.

Kamana has left many inscriptions, but as was mentioned before, these are all in fragments, which makes the translation of them into a coherent text impossible, with the exception of the partly preserved Cekke and A 24 inscriptions. Therefore, we have to rely, again, on the inscriptions of Yarairaisa, who says he had chosen Kamana for succession (A 7a) and adds, "Kamana was an immature boy who was crying for his dead father even on the day of his coronation (A 6.5).

After the death of Yarairaisa, for whom Kamana and his brothers had already made a resting place in the temple by their father's tomb (A 15b.3), Sastura became first minister, like his father Yarairaisa, to guide the young king.

In my opinion, the accession of Kamana was sometime around 770 BC, and the end of his reign, as we know from the Assyrians, falls in 738 BC, when his youngest brother, Pisiris, took over the kingdom.

In his Cekke inscription, Kamana informs us of an attack on one of his cities, Kamanaya, in the south, by a person named Warpata, which appears to be a play on the city name of Arpat. The date of this attack and the raising of the Cekke stela, in my opinion, fall in the middle of the 8th century BC. At the time the king of Arpat was a certain Mati'ilu, who had signed a treaty with Bar-ga'ya, the king of the Kaska people in the north. It appears the intention was that the Kaskan was to attack Tabal in the north and Mati'ilu, the southern lands, which was exactly what took place, and in both cases the assailants were defeated (for Bar-ga'ya and his attack on Tabal see Wasusaramimasa in the chapter devoted to Tabal, page 114ff).

Sastura

The name means 'grand admonisher'. His Classical Armenian recomposed name was Baz, which means an arm, such as the arm of the law, the arm of the king, executor of the law, etc.

Kamana, in the inscription of Cekke says: "I am Kamana who succeeded to the throne of Carchemish city, where Sastura is the country's overlord" — which means that Sastura runs the country. Kamana adds: "Sastura is my prime executor and adviser."

I am certain that Sastura was a son of Yarairaisa and was trained by him for the job. It is difficult to imagine an outsider acceding to the position of prime minister, particularly, when Yarairaisa had such influence on Kamana while he was a young king.

When Sargon II, in 717 BC, dethroned and exiled Pisiris, his family and his adherents to Assyria, Sastura had been dead for many years, which was the reason for his descendants to escape exile. Carchemish became an Assyrian governorship, but there was a want of local indigenous leading nobility, which position was filled in by the descendants of the House of Sastura. This matter will be dealt with in Chapter 15 when the proto-Armenians move to Urartu.

Sastura's Classical Armenian name of Baz is one of two names that have been repeated in Khorenatsi's prehistory. It appears first in Chapter 12 as Baz and again in Chapter 19 as Bazowk; both names meaning an arm.

Pisiris

The name means 'memory left behind by the thinker/truthful' (Astiruwa). The analysis of the name is as follows: 'pis' > 'his', has the sense of 'inheritor, son', but the main meaning is 'memory left behind'; 'ir' is the same stem found in the name of Ast*ir*uwa and also in Yara*ira*isa, which is due to the fact that the latter was connected to the king as his prime minister.

Pisiris was the youngest son of Astiruwa, which is confirmed by his recomposed Classical Armenian name of Husak (Khorenatsi 1.19). Husak means 'dear little last one', the 'hus' having the meanings of 'rearmost', and 'last' and is combined with the endearment diminutive suffix 'ak'.

In 738 BC, Kamana passed away, leaving Sastura to rule the country as caretaker. Sastura was not a king nor did he belong to the ruling dynasty of Astiruwa. Therefore, he chose Pisiris, the youngest son of Astiruwa, as the next king. In the A7 insctiption of Yarairaisa, Pisiris is the unnamed baby held in the arms of the queen.

The damaged inscription A22b does not divulge the name of its author; scholars are of the opinion that it belongs to this last king of Carchemish, which appears to be right. Unfortunately, this inscription does not give us much historical information, except to praise Sastura, which automatically confirms that Sastura was still the governor of the country and that it was Sastura that chose him to succeed to his father's throne.

Pisiris reigned until 717 BC, when Sargon II dethroned and exiled him to Assyria, accusing him of duplicity. By this time Sastura must have died, because his family escaped exile, whereas the king's retinue, according to Sargon's *Annals*, accompanied him to exile in Assyria.

THE KINGDOM OF GURGUM (MARASH)

The proto-Armenians flourish

The Paeonian settlements in Gurgum, with Marash as its main city, starts early in the 12th century BC like Carchemish. By the turn of the millennium, the proto-Armenian inhabitants of Marash set up a kingdom, which implies that further waves of Paeonian immigrants from the Balkans had joined the first settlers and had greatly increased the proto-Armenian population of the country.

Our knowledge of this most ancient proto-Armenian kingdom derives from three inscriptions; Marash VIII, Marash IV (Colossus) and Marash I (Lion), with gaps sometimes filled by Assyrian inscriptions, which do not set out to record the history of the Armenians, but are accounts of their own affairs; though from time to time they refer to the proto-Armenian cities as payers of tribute, vassals or enemies.

Khorenatsi, in his prehistory (book 1.21) confirms that our ancient kings used to be vassals and governors subordinate to the Assyrians, which is the reason for their names being included in the Assyrian records whence his information comes.

The rulers of Gurgum can be divided into two dynasties. We do not know whether there was any relationship between the last two kings and the seven before them. Certainly, there is a gap between the seventh king, Halparutiya III, and the next one, Tarkulara, which remains unfilled.

Ruler	Date	Source of attestation
Larazamasa I	975-955 (?)	Marash I; Marash VIII
Muwazisa	955-915 (?)	Marash I; Marash IV
Halparutiya I	915-885 (?)	Marash I
Muwazali	885-855 (?)	Marash I; Marash IV; Shalmaneser III
Halparutiya II	855-825 (?)	Marash I; Marash IV; Shalmaneser III
Larazamasa II	825-807 (?)	Marash I; Adad-nirari III
Halparutiya III	807-780 (?)	Marash I; Adad-nirari III
Tarkulara	745-712	Tiglath-Pileser III; Sargon II
Mutallu	712-711	Sargon II

Larazamasa I

This name means 'devoted to God' ('lara' > 'yara' = 'attached/joined' + 'za' = 'he/this one' + 'masa' = 'god'). This king is not remembered by Khorenatsi in his prehistory. Khorenatsi's list of names derives mainly from the Assyrian sources, which do not mention Larazamasa[5] the First. Khorenatsi's first name-list, that of the ancient kings, starts with Muwazisa/Manawaz, the son of Larazamasa the First (see the following name).

Larazamasa was a contemporary of Suhis I of Carchemish. These two rulers are the oldest proto-Armenian kings of south-eastern Anatolia (the country of Aram).

Larazamasa is the author of the archaic Marash VIII inscription, which is perhaps the oldest Armenian literary work. It is invaluable as a source of the archaic proto-Armenian language and history of its time. The inscription has many damaged and missing parts, but can still be understood. It starts with Larazamasa introducing himself and informing us of his father's and grandfather's names. They appear to have been priests as he himself was — his father's name was Muwazali, the same as the name of the fourth king of the dynasty.

According to the inscription, at the time when Larazamasa was the chief priest of the temple of the god Tark in Marash, there was no ruler. This situation prompted people from every part of the city to bear down upon the temple and carry him off to place him on the throne, proclaiming to the entire country and to the delight of the population, that from now on Larazamasa was to be king.

The inscription also tells us about an unnamed individual who arrived in the city, drunk too much wine and started a commotion. He was brought to justice, and interestingly, his punishment was to take certain quantity of lead to the temple (the word for 'lead' is 'kapar', the same as the present Armenian word). This same person returned with a group of men and started to kill people and set fire to properties, but in the end he was killed by being made to fall on a sword ('falling on a sword' is the expression used in the inscription, which we also see in the very last sentence of Carchemish A 15b.5 and Kululu II.1c). Larazamasa adds: "I nailed his body against a stone wall for all in the city to see."

Muwazisa

This name means 'fiery priest' ('muw' > 'mog' = 'a heathen priest' + 'az' = 'fire' + 'isa' = 'him, to this one'). His recomposed Classical Armenian name in Khorenatsi's prehistory (book I.12) was 'Manawaz' meaning a 'priest of fiery essence' ('man' = 'priest/magus' + 'aw' = 'essence of being' + 'az' = fire'), which correlates well with the archaic name; in fact, it could not have been a better interpretation.

Given that the Assyrians do not record this king's name, one might ask how Khorenatsi discovered it, since, as previously mentioned, his information derives from Assyrian sources. In this particular case it is obvious that Khorenatsi or his source had taken the name from the House of Manawaz in central Armenia. In my opinion, it was Khorenatsi's unknown source, who had recomposed all the names, so that they were understood by people of the Classical Armenian period, had used his knowledge of the distinguished past of the House of Muwazisa and translated the name as Manawaz, whose lands were called 'Hark'', meaning 'Land of the Fathers' — father, in this case has the sense of 'leader'. Because of the said distinguished past, Manawaz, in the archaic biblical style of oral history, was made a son of Hayk — see Part II.

Muwazisa's name is recorded in both the Marash I and IV inscriptions. It is remarkable that in the Marash IV inscription, the author, Halparutiya II, after naming his own father Muwazali, jumps to the name of his great-grandfather Muwazisa. Besides skipping over the name of his grandfather he does not even mention the name of the true primogenitor, Larazamasa I. I think this was due to the fact that Muwazisa was the most famous of all the kings of Gurgum, which must also be the reason for the entire dynasty and the later dukedom of Armenia being styled after him as Manawazians. It is ironical that we know nothing about this priest-king of Marash.

The Marash I inscription of Halparutiya III cites all the names of the dynasty going back six generations. Even in this inscription the name of Muwazisa is the only one designated 'the valorous'.

Scholars write this name as Muwanza, which is beyond my understanding. On what grounds, I wonder, do they tamper with such an archaic name, in view of the fact that the name of Muwazali, which they write correctly, has the same first two syllables of 'Muwaz'?

Halparutiya I
This name means either 'battering-ram of Rutiya' or 'in dialogue with Rutiya'. I think the first is the correct one. For

my explanation, and the reason for my preference, see my account of Halparutiya III below. The Assyrians do not mention this king. Khorenatsi mentions only one Hrant, who is the last king of this dynasty, Halparutiya III.

Muwazali

This name means 'acerbic fiery priest'. This explanation is confirmed by what his great-grandson, Halparutiya III, writes about him in the Marash I inscription. Of Muwazali he says: "His speech was full of fire." The Classical Armenian recomposed name of this king was 'Arbown' (Khorenatsi, Book I.19), which does not correlate with Muwazali, but has the same sense as the name Mutalli. Mutalli is the Assyrian version, which must be the demotic name of this king. Assyrians, as a rule, do not translate, but merely record the demotic names of the proto-Armenian kings, as we shall see in further examples. I find it odd that there is no correlation between the names Muwazali and Mutalli, except for the end words of both names, which are identical and have the meaning of 'acerbic'. However, the Assyrian version Mutalli and the Classical Armenian Arbown correlate perfectly, because Khorenatsi's names derive from the Assyrian sources.

Mutalli has the sense of 'a person of sharp speech having the innate ability to interpret dreams and discern the intention of the gods as if in a trance, or as if intoxicated', whereas Arbown has the sense of 'one in a trance without the need for intoxicants' (the word 'arbownk'' — the plural form — derives from 'arbown', meaning 'the age of puberty').

Shalmaneser III of Assyria in 858 BC, the first year of his campaign in the west, records that he drew near "to the cities of Mutalli the Gurgumean.[6] His tribute of silver, gold, wines and his daughter with costly dowry I received." In the Assyrian records of 853 BC (Shalmaneser III his sixth year), the name of the king of Gurgum is Halparutiya, which means that between 858 and 853 Muwazali had died and his son had succeeded him.

Halparutiya II

For the meaning of this name see Halparutiya I above,and for more details about its composition see Halparutiya III below. Assyrians mention this king as payer of tribute in the 6th year of Shalmaneser III in 853 BC.[7] In the Assyrian inscriptions, or rather in their translation, the name appears as Qalparuda/ K'alparuda. Khorenatsi does not know this king, but mentions both his father Arbown and his son P'arokh (Larazamasa II). The Marash IV (Colossus) inscription belongs to this king. Only a part of the inscription has survived. The end is missing and a few lines are damaged.

From what he writes one can see that he was truly clever and pragmatic king. He informs us of the death of the ruler of the city of Hiraka, when an unnamed person decides to usurp power, which act is described as rebellion. He expresses his relief that the rebellion was confined to the city of Hiraka, even though the person responsible for it had also pillaged and burned the city of Ilawasa. Obviously the unnamed rebel knows the severity of his misdeeds, and in order to avoid retribution shuts himself up in the city of Hiraka. Halparutiya, in his turn besieges the city, and forces the rebels to hand over the loot they had taken from the city of Ilawasa. In recompense, and to his delight, the leader of the rebellion surrenders the city of Hiraka to him. His clever move was of benefit to the kingdom, because from this time onwards Hiraka is incorporated in it. He adds, "later this rebel became a priest and came to see me".

Larazamasa II

This name was explained above as 'devoted to God' — see the first king of the same name above for more details. His demotic name, which the Assyrians mention, though indirectly, was Palalam,[8] on the occasion of a border dispute between Gurgum and Kummukh, at the time of Adad-nirari III, when the Assyrians acted as intermediaries and decided in favour of Kummukh. At the time, Halparutiya was king of Marash, whom the Assyrians call 'Qalparuda (III) son of Palalam'.

The name Palalam, the Assyrian version of this king's name, has the same sense as Larazamasa. The analysis of the name is 'pal' > 'hal' = 'attached' + 'alam'= 'take salt together'; in other words, the king is attached to god and takes salt with him, which is the archaic way of saying that the king is in communion with the gods. This archaic compound of 'alam' is still used in the same sense, but has a new composition of 'ałakits'' (the 'am' = 'together/attached' has been changed to 'kits'' which has the identical meanings — 'al' and 'ał' are the same word meaning 'salt', which means 'friendship, attached in a comradely fashion'). In Khorenatsi's prehistory (book I.12) this king is referred to as P'arokh, which derives from the Assyrian version of the name of Palalam — Khorenatsi does not know the name Larazamasa. P'arokh means 'blessed diligence'; the diligence referring to his serving the god. The founder of the Gurgum dynasty was also called Larazamasa, but we cannot ascribe to him the demotic name of Palalam, as we do not know whether there was such a demotic name at that period.

Halparutiya III .

This name and my preference for the meaning 'the battering-ram of Rutiya' were mentioned above. The Assyrians mention him as Qalparuda and K'alparuda (depending whose translation one is reading) in the year 805 BC, at the time of Adad-nirari III. This king is the only Halparutiya whom Khorenatsi refers to in Book I.19 as Hrant, which is the Classical Armenian version of the Assyrian rendering of the 'ruda' of Qalparuda. The Halparutiya II mentioned by the Assyrians in the inscriptions of Shalmaneser III (853 BC) Khorenatsi does not know, perhaps due to the fact that the compiler of the proto-Armenian name-list might have been under the impression that the first ruler under this name of 853 was the same person recorded in 805, which may, also, be the reason why in the name-lists there is only one Hrant mentioned.

Qalparuda transcribes to the Armenian as K'alparuda (Q > K'), which means the initial 'H' of the proto-Armenian name must have been pronounced as 'Kh' > Khalparutia. The transcription of the Assyrian name into Armenian confirms the meaning 'the battering ram of Rutiya' as follows: 'khal/qal' > 'k'al' (after the sixth century the 'l' became 'ł', therefore 'k'ał') = 'ram' + 'pa' > 'baχ' = 'to batter, pound' + 'Rutiya' = the proto-Armenian rendering of the name of the god Runzas.

The name Hrant, assigned by Khorenatsi to the Assyrian Qalparuda cannot be explained in the Armenian language in spite of much scholarly effort. Hrant identifies the name of the god Rutiya with the Assyrian 'ruda'. Most probably the compiler of the Classical Armenian name had not understood the Qalpa part of the name (there is another example of this in the name of Wasusaramimasa, which the Assyrians had written as Uasusarma, and the compiler of the name-list had armenicised it as Harma, which is only the Assyrian rendering of the name of the god Sarma). In the Armenian language there are no indigenous words starting with 'r', therefore to most of the borrowed words starting with 'r' there is usually an added initial 'h'; hence the name Ruda > Hrant, which is also written as Hrand.

Halparutiya III is the author of Marash I (Lion) inscription. We owe him the full list of the names of the Gurgum dynasty up to his own time. The inscription consists of 6 lines, of which the first three are devoted to the Gurgum genealogy. In line 4 he recounts how he succeeded to the throne. It is interesting to note the present Armenian custom of welcoming dignitaries with bread and salt. It appears that salt had been added to the formality in later years, if we are to take note of what Halparutiya says: "The court usher came to me with a piece of bread and told me that as from now I was king, because my father had chosed me before he died." The last part of line 6 refers to a covetous person who arrived with a gang in order to snatch the throne. "He begrudged me for being my father's choice," he says, but exactly at this point, unfortunately, the inscription is damaged and the continuation, which should have been on an accompanying slab, is missing.

I do not know whether it is a coincidence or due to some reasons beyond the control of the Gurgumeans that, like with Carchemish and Tabal (Tabal will be referred to later), there is an intermission in the rulership of Marash in the first half of 8th century BC. Also, for that period there are no records at all, either indigenous or Assyro-Babylonian. Because of this dark period it is not known how and when Halparutiya, the last of his line, met his end. At the start of the second half of the same century, some glimmer of light is thrown on the affairs of this kingdom by Tiglath-Pileser III and Sargon II of Assyria.

Tarkulara

This name means 'thunder took a girl (as wife)' as follows: 'tark' = 'thunder' + 'ul' = 'youngster, kid' + 'ara' = 'took, carried'.

Khorenatsi's prehistory does not mention this king, but the Assyrians (Tiglath-Pileser III) record him as tribute payer in the years 743, 738 and 732 BC.[9] Sargon II, also mentions him in the year 711 BC[10] in connection with his death at the hands of his son, Mutallu, in 712 BC. The parricide may have its explanation in the name Tarkulara. It may well be that marrying a teenager might have prejudiced Mutallu's chances of succession, and he had to act in order to safeguard his interest.

Mutallu

This name means, if it is correct that it ends with 'U' and not 'I' as was the case with Mutalli (Muwazali), 'good-natured person in a trance' ('mut' > 'moyn' = 'in a trance, interpreter of dreams, to submerge' + 'allu' > 'ału' = 'good-natured')

As mentioned above, in 712 BC Mutallu murdered his father, which was either against the wishes of Sargon of Assyria, or was a good pretext for the latter to dethrone Mutallu and make the country of Gurgum a governorship. Whatever the reason, Mutallu was apprehended and exiled to Assyria, putting an end to indigenous rule of the country.

Thus ends the long line of kings of Gurgum (Marash) never to be resumed. It appears, as we shall see in the next part, the House of Muwazisa, that is the descendants of the first dynasty, again became the leading noble House with responsibilities for the proto-Armenian population of Gurgum. This house will lead the population of Aram to Urartu in early 6th century BC, where they will become known as the House of Manawazians in central Armenia, and their lands will be called Hark', 'Land of the Fathers'.

THE KINGDOM OF MELID (MALATYA)

The oldest settlers

The proto-Armenian settlement in this part of Anatolia may be the oldest. The Paeonians had come from the Balkans as one of the members of the Mushki coalition, and at the time were the most numerous of the immigrants.[11] However, Melid as a large centre of proto-Armenian settlement was soon overtaken in size by Carchemish and Gurgum, which may be inferred from the fact that the Melitineans did not manage to seize power until the end of the 9th century BC, whereas the Carchemish and Gurgum proto-Armenian rulerships started in the first half of the 10th century.

The proto-Armenian population of Melid and Tabal grew to appreciable size only after the arrival of the Pelagonian Paeonians, together with the Phrygians, at the end of the 9th century BC,[12] which coincides with the accession of the first king, Shakhu, recorded by Khorenatsi in Book I.12 as 'Shara'.

There may have been other proto-Armenian kings prior to Shakhu, but these are not recorded in Khorenatsi's prehistory of the Armenians. Some fragments of hieroglyphic inscriptions do record names of rulers, such as Satara (Inscn. Malatya I), Suwairami (Inscn. Malatya III), and the Assyrian inscriptions mention an Allumari (Tiglath-Pileser I) and Lalli

(Shalmaneser III). Of these, Satara and Suwairami may be proto-Armenian names, but Allumari and Lalli seem more of Aramaean provenance, although all the names are explainable in the Armenian language.

The kings of Melid are divided into two dynasties and two individuals. The first dynasty is that of Shakhu, Khelaruada and Sulumal, followed by the two individuals named Gunzinanu and Tarkunazi followed in turn by a short dynasty of father and son named Mugallu and ...ussi, whose hegemony also included Tabal. The Assyrians record these last two names as kings of Tabal since at the time of these kings Tabal and Melid were unified under one rule. It is a fact that Mugallu started as king of Melid and that a while later, after the mysterious disappearance of Ishkallu of Tabal he extended his kingdom to include the lands belonging to the latter. This is the main reason for including Mugallu and his son ...ussi both among the kings of Melid and of Tabal.

Ruler	Date	Source of Attestation
Shakhu/Shadawale	790?; 783; 750	Menua; Argishti I; Sarduri II
Khelaruada	783; 750	Argishti I; Sarduri II
Sulumal	738; 732	Tiglath-Pileser III
Gunzinanu	728?; 717?	Tiglath-Pileser III; Sargon II
Tarkunazi	717?; 712	Sargon II
Mugallu	675; 668	Esarhaddon; Ashurbanipal
...ussi	640?	Ashurbanipal

Shakhu

This is one of the few names that can be double checked. Menua's (810-786 BC) inscription, cited by Diakonoff (Note 119, pp.199), quoting Melikishvili's translation, reads: ". . . in the same year I gathered my warriors, and they took from the (-)uan country the town of Shurishile, the town of Tarhigama, the town of (-)tura on the side towards the (dynasty) of Shadawale, (and) from the bank of the River (Me)le, etc." This Shadawale is the same person as Sulekhauali referred to by Barnett,[13] though Barnett's reading of the name has been rejected.

Shadawale means 'very mean' and 'avaricious' ('šad' = 'very' + 'awal' > 'agah' = 'mean'). The name of this king also appears in the inscriptions of Argishti I (786-764 BC) and Sarduri II (764-735 BC) as Shakhu in the phrase "Khelaruada son of Shakhu".[14] Shakhu means 'usurer/extortionist' ('shaχ' is no longer used, since the Iranian loan word 'vashχ', of the same meaning, has replaced it), which correlates with the Shadawale version of this king's name.

The Classical Armenian recomposition of this name in Khorenatsi's Book I.12 was 'Shara', which has a similar sense (it is not known whether the word 'shariad', meaning 'excessive interest and tax', derives from the name Shara or the other way round). Irrespective of this meaning, the name Shara has acquired a euphemistic interpretation of 'gluttonous/ gormandizer', which is seen in the most ancient aphorism quoted by Khorenatsi: "If you have the appetite of Shara, we do not have the stores of Shirak", in other words Shara stands for gluttony (when a guest overeats) and the district named, allegedly after Shara, as Shirak was one of the most productive of northern Armenia.

The Assyrians do not mention the name of this king, therefore, Khorenatsi's name must derive from this aphorism or the name of the Sophene dukedom of Shahians, which Khorenatsi correctly interconnects, asserting a few times that the Shahians were the descendants of Shara, after whom the district of Shirak was named. The district of Shirak used to belong to the margraves of the northern borders of Armenia known as Gusharids, about whom Khorenatsi says that they too were the descendants of Shara.

The descendants of Shara and the Shahian dukedom will be

examined in Part III. Suffice to say that the name Shahian is a later euphemism, because 'shah' means legitimate profit derived from any transaction, whereas we have already seen what 'shaχ' means.

Khelaruada

The meaning of this name is 'noble capable male' ('khel' > 'gel' = 'noble' + 'aru' = 'male' + 'ad' = 'capable, able') depending on the sense of the word 'aru' (male), which we do not see in any other name. If 'aru' is a titular of a king then the explanation is correct, but if it stands for one of its other senses, such as 'brave, valiant, valorous and gallant', then the meaning becomes 'noble brave and capable'. 'Aru' is used in the Topada inscription, line 1, in the phrase "wa KING-ti sa ARU zi" ('because he had become a brave king'); but in this phrase 'ARU' is not part of the name of the person referred to.

His Classical Armenian recomposed name, in Khorenatsi Book I.19, was Vstamkar, meaning 'noble and wholly capable'. Vstamkar is the compound of 'vst' > 'vest' ('vest' is a loan from the Iranian and has replaced 'khel') = 'noble' + 'am' = 'wholly, completely' + 'kar' = 'capable' ('kar' is a synonym of 'ad'). Khelaruada was the son of Shakhu as Argishti and Sarduri testify.

Argishti in his fourth campaign attacked Melid Kummanu and according to his inscription took some 30,000 prisoners of whom he settled 6,000 in the north-east of Urartu in his newly fortified city of Erebuni (present Erevan).[15]

Sarduri II in his first campaign in the west attacked the lands of Melid Kummanu and annexed nine fortress cities to Urartu. A subdued Khelaruada had to pay a large tribute of gold, silver, cattle and valuables, beside agreeing to an annual tribute. Sarduri also took a great number of prisoners and settled them in the north-east of Urartu, as Argishti had done before him, in order to create a buffer zone against the belligerent tribes of Etiu, Uelikukhi, Eriakhi and Abiliani.[16] The total of displaced proto-Armenians, between Menua,

Argishti and Sarduri may have been in excess of 75,000 persons; these were the first proto-Armenian minority of Urartu.

Despite his tribulations and the burden of tribute to Urartu, Khelaruada appears to have had a very long reign and, as we infer from his name, he was well liked by the population of Melid.

Sulumal

The name of this king means 'radiance of goodness' ('sul' > 'ts'ol' = 'radiance, brilliance, shine' + 'um' = 'who is' + 'al' = 'salt', meaning 'lovely, sweet, good' — the proto-Armenian endearing diminutive suffix). This name is recorded in the inscriptions of Tiglath-Pileser III of Assyria. We do not have any indigenous sources to verify it, other than its Classical Armenian recomposition in Khorenatsi's *History* (book I.12) as 'Gełam' and 'Gełamay', which mean 'wholly noble' ('geł' = 'noble,' this is the same as the 'khel' of Khelaruada + 'am' = 'wholly, completely'). It is not known exactly when Sulumal succeeded to his father's throne, neither is it known when his reign came to an end. In Tiglath-Pileser's inscriptions his name appears as a tributary for the years 738 and 732 BC.[17]

Sulumal was one of the members of the north Syrian coalition of various city-states against the Assyrian threat, but it appears he was left on the throne in exchange for a heavy tribute imposed on Melid by the Assyrians. A few years after 732 BC, the last date he was mentioned in the Assyrian inscriptions of Tiglath-Pileser III, Sulumal was either dethroned or died a natural death (considering that his son did not succeed him, I think, it is safe to assume that he was dethroned by Tiglath-Pileser III), which limits his reign to before 727 BC, the death of Tiglath-Pileser. His successor was a certain Gunzinanu.

As we shall see in Part III, the descendants of Sulumal became known as the 'Royal House of Gełs' in later Armenia.

Gunzinanu

This name means 'vainglorious leopard' ('G' = emphatic suffix + 'unz' = 'leopard' + 'inan' = 'nothing, devoid, vain, empty'), or 'leopard devoid', which gives the sense of 'a person named leopard who lacks the courage and the spirit of that animal'. This demotic name must have been given to him because he had no influence on state matters and was a mere tool of the Assyrians.

His Classical Armenian recomposed name was Ĕndzak ('ĕndz' = 'leopard', this is the 'unz' of the proto-Armenian name + 'ak' = an endearing diminutive suffix), which has a euphemistic interpretation as 'good old leopard'. His name suggests that he was not greatly admired by the people, which might have been due to his replacing the much loved Sulumal.

The date of his succession, like the date of Sulumal's dethronement or death, is not known; but it certainly had to be after 732 and before 728 BC. Sargon II of Assyria dethroned Gunzinanu, but, again, we do not know exactly when. It is possible that this event took place in the fifth year of Sargon's reign, which fell in 717 BC, the year when Pisiris of Carchemish was exiled to Assyria. However, in the case of Gunzinanu, Sargon does not mention an exile, all he records is: "I drove Gunzinanu out of the country."[18] Unfortunately, the Armenian traditions recorded by Khorenatsi do not tell us anything about Gunzinanu, as is the case with most of the other rulers. However, we find the name of Ĕndzak recorded in Book I.19, for which we must be grateful.

Tarkunazi

This name means 'thunder devoid of fire' ('tark' = 'thunder' + 'un' = 'devoid, empty, without' + 'az' = fire, flame). His recomposed Classical Armenian name was Tork' Angeł, meaning 'Tark the Ignoble' ('Tork'' > 'Tark' = chief god's name meaning also 'thunder' + 'angeł' = 'not noble'). See 'khel' of Khelaruada and 'geł' of Gełam: both have been translated as 'noble'/'vest', but the word 'geł' has also the meanings of beautiful, handsome, fair, which is the main reason why this name has been misunderstood.

Khorenatsi mentions this name outside of the three name-lists in Book II.8, but he also makes a reference to Angeł Tun (House of Angełs), the seat of the descendants of Tarkunazi in Armenia, in Book I.23.

When Sargon dethroned Gunzinanu, Tarkunazi was his choice as another client ruler of Melid. The date may have been 717 BC. However, a few years later, in 712 to be exact, the 10th year of Sargon's reign, Tarkunazi was accused of duplicity. In Sargon's words "he directed perfidious messages against the land of Assyria".[19] Melid was attacked by the Assyrians, which forced Tarkunazi to take refuge in the fortified city of Togarmah (House of T'orgom — in Assyrian, Til-garimmu).[20] The people of Togarmah, in the face of the Assyrian presence, and in order to avoid the wrath of Sargon, surrendered Tarkunazi and his followers to the Assyrians, who exiled them in iron fetters to Nineveh.[21] Sargon gave the city of Melid to Mutallu of Kummukh,[22] but the rest of the country, the large district of Kummanu, was placed under Assyrian governorship. Thus the line of the old kings of Melid Kummanu, Khorenatsi's first generation appearing in his first name-list of Hayk's progeny, ends with Tarkunazi, and until the time of Esarhaddon of Assyria there are no indigenous rulers.

It is now understandable why this king, Tarkunazi, was given the name of 'thunder devoid of fire'. In history he was known as a powerful giant of a man, and yet in the face of the enemy he run away, leaving Melid to the mercy of the Assyrians. Sargon boasts that he "crushed Melid like a pot".[23] The Classical Armenian recomposition of the name agrees with this interpretation, though the name has been misunderstood and most scholars explain it differently, following later bards and minstrels. Even Khorenatsi, who infers from the 'Angeł' part of the new name that Tarkunazi was an ugly, lame and flat-nosed giant.

Much has been written about this ancient ruler, both in

olden days and in recent times. However, all such literature is based on Khorenatsi's story, and none of the writers knew exactly who Tork' Angeł really was and why was he called Angeł. Some scholars, because of their unawareness of the facts, have changed even the epithet Angeł to 'Angł'.

Mugallu

This is the Assyrian rendering of the name and there are no indigenous sources to confirm it (the proto-Armenian rendering of the name would have been Muzala). The meaning of the name is rather curious, but in agreement with history and with what Khorenatsi writes in Book I.14. The name has the sense of 'promoted/progressed good natured person' ('mug' > 'moz' = 'promoted, progressed, mighty, strong' + 'allu' = 'good-natured'). His Classical Armenian recomposed name was 'Mshak', which means 'cultivator' — this is the same as the Greek name Γεωργος/George.

According to Khorenatsi, Mshak was entrusted with the districts of Caesarea Mazacca (today's Kayseri) in Tabal, which is in accord with what we know of him; hence the promoted or the progressed part of the ancient name of Mugallu. He was also instructed to teach the population of those parts the Armenian language, hence, Khorenatsi concludes, his Classical Armenian epithet of 'cultivator'.

It is not known when Mugallu came to power. Esarhaddon (680-669 BC) of Assyria records a campaign against Mugallu of Melid in 675 BC. Obviously, Assyria was very concerned with the progress this king had made, which can also be noticed in Esarhaddon's questions to the oracle of Shamash,[24] which unwittingly reveals this concern, because, at the time Mugallu of Melid and Ishkallu of Tabal were pursuing an anti-Assyrian policy.[25] These facts also confirm that after thirty-odd years of Assyrian domination of Melid Kummanu and Tabal, early in the 7th century BC, both of these countries had secured their independence.

By 668 BC Mugallu's suzerainty had extended to include Tabal due to the unexplained disappearance of Ishkallu. At the time both countries were in turmoil due to the presence of the Cimmerian hordes under their chief Lygdamis (Dugdamme). This must have been the main reason for Mugallu's embassy to Ashurbanipal (668-627 BC) of Assyria in 668. The Assyrian inscriptions of Ashurbanipal record that: "Mugallu, king of Tabal, who had addressed words of enmity to the kings, my fathers, brought a daughter with a large dowry to Nineveh, to serve as my concubine, and kissed my feet. On Mugallu I laid a yearly tribute of large horses."[26] Ashurbanipal's words may be true, because at the time Mugallu had to be on good terms with Assyrians in the face of the Cimmerian menace. In 652 BC the Cimmerians under Lygdamis attacked Lydia, whose king, Gyges, perished in the fight. This latter event proves that Mugallu was right to be apprehensive of the Cimmerians, and his goodwill towards Ashurbanipal was well conceived.

The Assyrians refer to Mugallu, and after him to his son ...ussi, as kings of Tabal though there is no evidence that the hegemony of these two kings had ceased to include Melid. Mugallu started his career as king of Melid, and for this reason I have placed him, and his son after him, among the rulers of Melid, although both of these kings will also be included among the list of rulers of Tabal.

...ussi

The first part of the name of this king of Melid and Tabal is erased from the Assyrian inscriptions, perhaps in retaliation for his anti-Assyrian conduct. In fact, the Assyrians, that is Ashurbanipal, ascribe the death of ...ussi in a palace fire as devine retribution.[27] Who was ...ussi? We know for certain that he was the son of Mugallu, but what was his real name? In my mind there is no doubt that he was the Anushawan of Khorenatsi's writing, mentioned in Book I.19-20.

The name Anushawan means 'without place of rest and

memory' ('an' = 'without', a negative prefix equal to the English 'un-' + 'ush' = 'memory, remembrance, intellect' + 'awan' = 'resting/habitation place'). The '...ussi' ending of the archaic name is the same as the 'ush' of the Classical Armenian recomposition — this '...ussi' or 'ush' may be due to the fact that the Assyrians had erased his name. Considering the Assyrian attitude towards this king, and the fact that he died in a palace fire, one could understand that he could be described as having had no resting place. Therefore the king known only as ...ussi, must be the Anushawan of the Armenian tradition preserved by Khorenatsi, who adds that "this Anushawan encountered much contempt from the Assyrians" — which also happens to be historically true.

The death of ...ussi, in the last years of Ashurbanipal, marked the end of the last kingdom of Tabal and Melid, which was not long before the time when Nineveh, the capital city of Assyria, was itself destroyed by the Medes, after which both Melid and Tabal, being to the east of the River Halis, fell under the hegemony of the Medes. But this is also near enough to the time when the proto-Armenians of the country of Aram (except Kummukh and Cilicia) moved into the highlands of Urartu, which in due course was to become known as Armenia.

CHAPTER 7

THE KINGDOM OF KUMMUKH

A productive country

Kummukh was the Assyrian name for this productive country, which later became known as the Roman Commagene. From the Taurus mountains (the Malatyan range) to the north it stretched all the way down the western bank of the Euphrates, south to Carchemish; Gurgum (Marash) was to the west of Kummukh.

The Assyrians refer to this country and the main city as Kummukh, as they do in the case of Carchemish; it is therefore possible that the capital city was called Kummukh and that the name of the country derives from it; otherwise, we do not have a city name as such.

Kummukh was essentially a Hurrian country with a scattering of Hittites in the main centres. The proto-Armenian population must have slowly penetrated this state, starting from the 12th century BC, until the time when they were able to initiate or take over the rulership, and run it as a proto-Armenian state. It is not known if Kummukh had a ruler prior to the first king we know of, the proto-Armenian Qatazilu, who belongs to the first half of the 9th century BC.

Overshadowed by the brilliance of Carchemish, some 120 km south of Arsameia, and of Melid, some 65 km directly to the north, Kummukh appears to have been an isolated area of south-eastern Anatolia until as a kingdom it became a tributary of the Assyrians.

Judging from the names of two kings, Kundashpi and Kushtashpi, Kummukh must have been a great centre for horse breeding. The country had a wealth of minerals, too, though we do not know to what extend they had exploited these. Certainly, there was an abundance of gold, silver and copper in the state to satisfy Assyrian greed.

The names of four proto-Armenian kings and a queen with a non-Armenian husband are known; but due to the scarcity of genealogical material and of hieroglyphic inscriptions in general, it is not known for certain whether these kings represented a dynasty, a continuous line with a break half way through, or whether these were unrelated individuals who had managed to succeed to the throne. One thing, however, is certain; they were all proto-Armenians, with the exception of the said queen's husband; and all are recorded in the prehisitory of the Armenians by Khorenatsi (Book I.19); even though, in the cases of Kundashpi and Kushtashpi, the explanation of their names is not as straightforward as with the other names.

Ruler	Date	Source of attestation
Qatazilu	866; 858; 857	Ashurnasirpal II; Shalmaneser III
Kundashpi	853-834	Shalmaneser III
Ushpilulume	805; 773	Adad-nirari III; Shalmaneser IV
Queen Panamuwatis		By her own Commagene Inscription
Kushtashpi	750; 743	Sarduri II; Tiglath-Pileser III
Mutallu	711; 708	Sargon II

Four hieroglyphic inscriptions have so far been found in Kummukh, of which the longest belongs to the queen, Panamuwatis; the other three are short fragments which impart no historical information.[28] Even the long inscription relating to the queen is devoid of any historical content, as it is in essence no more than a eulogy on the occasion of the death of her father-in-law, a certain Azami (a Hurrian name).

The mountain of Nemrud (Nemrut Dağ, altitude 2,150 metres — this should not be confused with the other mountain of the same name to the west of Lake Van), overlooking Arsameia (Eski Kahta), was the holy sanctuary of Kummukh where the kings and princes had been customarily buried.[29] It is now remembered as the sanctuary of Antiochus I (69-36 BC) and contains huge statues of the Greek divinities. According to Khorenatsi, even Sargon II (Bel) was buried on this mountain by his slayer, Eshpai (Hayk), and after the burial the place became known as 'cemeteries' (in the plural).[30] Eshpai (Hayk) had provided Sargon with a burial fit for a king, though this does not agree with what Isaiah says in the Old Testament (Chapter 14), without disclosing the king's name.

Qatazilu

This name has been translated into Greek as Asteropaeus (*Iliad* XXI), which has the same meaning of 'lightning' as the proto-Armenian name Qatazilu.

The name can be analysed in two ways:

a) 'Qat' > 'kay' ('there is') + 'az' ('fire') + 'ilu' ('overflowing') = 'there is overflowing fire'.
b) 'Qataz' > 'kaytz' ('spark') + 'ilu' ('overflowing') = 'overflowing with sparks'.

Therefore, in both cases the explanation is 'lightning'.

In Khorenatsi's history, Book I.19, this name has been recomposed as Ampak, which means 'source of lightning' (the modern Armenian meaning of 'amp' is 'cloud', but in the old language it also meant 'lightning', which can be discerned from a few inherited compounds, such as 'ampahar' ('struck by lightning'), for which the modern word is 'kaytzaknahar' (literally, 'struck by the source of sparks'). Therefore, the modern Armenian equivalent of Qatazilu is 'Kaytzak' ('lightning' — 'source of sparks').

Qatazilu was a contemporary of both Ashurnasirpal II and Shalmaneser III of Assyria. He was also a contemporary of Sangara of Carchemish and Muwazali of Gurgum.

In 866 BC, though Kummukh was not under attack, Qatazilu paid tribute to Ashurnasirpal, while the latter was in the neighbouring country of Khuzirina.[31] His name is also mentioned in 858-857 BC as a tributary to Shalmaneser III. It is most likely that the next king, Kundashpi, was his son.

Kundashpi

The meaning of this name is 'one who has regiments of cavalry' ('kund' = 'regiment, group' + 'ashpi' = 'cavalry, horse'). This name has been recomposed in Classical Armenian era as Vashtak ('vasht' = 'regiment, group' + 'ak' = 'source'), which we find in Khorenatsi's prehistory Book I.19.

The name Kundashpi, as well as Kushtashpi, is comprehensible to any Armenian with secondary school education, because the words 'gund ('kund'), 'kusht' and 'asp' ('ashpi') are part of the modern Armenian vocabulary. However, these words are not indigenous. It has been accepted for a long time that these words were loans from the Pahlavi or Old Persian language;[32] and yet we find them in use a thousand years before the Armenians had contacts with Pahlavi, which presents us with a puzzle. Why should a proto-Armenian king have an Indo-Aryan name, and where do these words come from? It is interesting to note that even the recomposed names of these kings do not use indigenous words.

The restructured Indo-European stem for a horse is *ek'wo-, which in Armenian would become 'asu'.[33] This is confirmed in the inscriptions wherein horse and horseman are called 'asu' and 'asuwa' (see the Topada inscription, any line; one of the most interesting lines [5] says: "pawa tá mana ASU-ti" = "I made the rounds (inspected) of the cavalry.") To ignore the indigenous words and instead to use Indo-Aryan for the names of these two kings, I think, might have been to ingratiate the Hurrian population (as we shall see below, this king's daughter married a Hurrian prince). The Hurrians of the Mitanni empire had acquired Indo-Aryan words from their governing elite, whose names had Indo-Aryan etymologies,[34] which means that such words had already been incorporated in the Hurrian language. This claim is further supported by the Kikkuli Text for the training of horses found in Boğazköy which, though written by a Hurrian, contains Indo-Aryan words.[35]

Kundashpi must have succeeded to the throne of Kummukh some time between 857 and 853 BC, because he is shown as a payer of tribute to Shalmaneser III in the year 853.[36] His name is included in the list of south-eastern Anatolian rulers as tributaries from 853 to 834 BC.

Panamuwatis and Ushpilulume

This is a husband and wife team; the combined names tell us an interesting story. It is obvious from the explanation of the names, that the queen, Panamuwatis, was a daughter of Kundashpi and in direct line to the throne of the country. Panamuwatis, the proto-Armenian princess, married a Hurrian prince by the name of Suppiluliumas, which was resented by the proto-Armenian population, hence his demotic name of Ushpilulume. This name derives from the Assyrian inscriptions.[37] As we have seen, the Assyrians record, in the main, the demotic names of the rulers of south-eastern Anatolia. Khorenatsi does not mention either of these two names in his pre-history, which means that the compiler or compilers of the name-lists knew the meaning of these two names and were aware that the king's name was not of proto-Armenian provenance.

Panamuwatis: The name means 'great lady married to this wind' ('pan' > 'han' ('great lady, grandmother') +

'am' ('together, married to') + 'uw' ('person, soul, being') + 'atis' > 'ayis' > 'ays' ('wind, breeze') — we see the 'atis' > 'ayis' stem in the name of Tuwatis (Aramayis).

Ushpilulume: This name means 'where did this scar swim from?' ('ushpi' > 'spi' (pronounced 'ĕspi') = 'scar, blemish' + 'lul' > 'loł' = 'to swim, to take a bath' + 'ume' = 'where from'), the swim having the sense of 'sneak, slip-in, penetrate'.

Ushpilulume was an Assyrian client king, and in 805 BC he asked for and received Assyrian support in connection with a border dispute with Gurgum.[38] Adad-nirari III acted as intermediary in settling the dispute between the two kingdoms in favour of Kummukh. Ushpilulume is also mentioned by Shalmaneser IV (781-772 BC) when the *turtanu* (Assyrian governor and military commander) Shamshi-ilu, confirmed the boundary which was drawn by Adad-nirari. Of course, all this cost Kummukh a lot of gold too, which was readily available as it is possible that Kummukh was an important source of the metal.

Panamuwatis, the proto-Armenian princess, has left a long inscription known as the Boybeypinarı I, II, III and IV, which has been completely misunderstood. This inscription is both a eulogy and record of what she had done for her father-in-law Azami, who had died at a ripe old age. This inscription will be fully translated in the companion volume to this study.

Kushtashpi

This name means 'flanks full with cavalry' ('kusht' = 'flank, side' + 'ashpi' = 'cavalry, horse'). In the Classical Armenian era it is replaced by the ready-to-hand Iranian name of Shawarsh, which means 'one who has black horses', the emphasis being on male horses ('shaw' = 'black' + 'arsh' = 'horse'). This name appears in Khorenatsi's Book I.19.

Sarduri of Urartu attacked Kummukh in 750 BC, when Kushtashpi capitulated, and besides paying a tribute, also joined the anti-Assyrian alliance of various states under the leadership of Urartu.[39] Tiglath-Pileser's offensive of 743 destroyed this alliance,[40] and once again Kummukh was back in the Assyrian camp. It appears that Kushtashpi was forgiven, which must have cost him much gold and silver.

Mutallu

The meaning of this name was discussed above under Mutallu of Gurgum (Marash) — see page 90. This is the second Mutallu name that does not appear in Khorenatsi's prehisitory; I am unable to say why. Khorenatsi mentions only one Mutalli (not Mutallu) as Arbown, who is Muwazali of Gurgum (Marash).

In 711 BC the country of Kummukh was enlarged by Sargon's presenting Mutallu with the city of Melid after the dethronement of Tarkunazi.[41] Obviously a large tribute must have been imposed on Mutallu, who withheld his contribution, and thus roused Sargon's anger. Sargon denounced Mutallu, saying: "Mutallu of Kummukh, who did not fear the name of the great gods . . . Meliddu, his stronghold, which I had put under his rule . . . withheld tribute . . . his wife, sons, daughters, he forsook, and fled alone and was seen no more."[42] In 708 BC, Sargon sent his generals against Kummukh, when the country with all its wealth passed into Assyrian hands, and a large part of the population was uprooted and resettled on the borders of Elam.[43] As from 708 BC Kummukh remained an Assyrian province.

The fall of Nineveh (612 BC) and the ascendancy of Babylon changed the political situation, and in the time of Nabuchadrezzar Kummukh became a Babylonian province. The Babylonians built fortifications overlooking Urartu. Under these circumstances the proto-Armenian population of the country could not participate in the move to the Urartian highlands. Eventually, in the first half of the 3rd century BC, they were able to set up a new kingdom of Kummukh and Sophene.

CHAPTER 8

THE KINGDOM OF TABAL

A multitude of minor kingdoms

Tabal was the largest and the most complex of the south-eastern Anatolian countries. Because of its size it contained a multitude of minor kingdoms, which were vassals of the "great" kings of Tabal. Our information derives from the Assyrian inscriptions, which record the names of the various rulers and the city-states with which they were in conflict or had imposed tribute on them. The indigenous hieroglyphic inscriptions do not tell us much about matters relating to boundaries, affairs of state or political and economic conditions. They are, in the main, personal records of achievements and grievances.

A rough sketch of the political boundaries can be drawn on the basis of the Assyrian texts, which mention the various cities and their neighbouring countries.

To the east of Tabal we find the kingdom of Melid Kummanu, to the south-east, the two kingdoms of Kummukh and Gurgum, to the south the whole of Cilicia, which was itself subdivided into various kingdoms, Phrygia in the west and the Kaska lands to the north. In modern terms Tabal would contain the western part of the modern district of Sivas, the districts of Kayseri, Nevşehir and Niğde, and in the earlier days of Tuatte and Kikki, also the northern part of Cilicia Campestris, the modern city of Kozan (Sis) and its districts — the city of Kozan itself was the ancient Sissu, named after Kikki, son of Tuatte.

The earlier existence of a monolithic Hittite empire in these lands could not have served as a paradigm for the newcomers, the Paeonians/proto-Armenians, who most probably would have had no knowledge of it. The newcomers would have continued to live in the only manner they were used to in the Balkans, which was in small cities with tribal chiefs, whom in Anatolia they learned to call kings (Tuwa), a word, most probably, borrowed from the Aramaeans.

It is remarkable that we know the names of the minor subordinate city-states, but not that of the capital city where the "great" king and his court resided. Some scholars are of the opinion that the present village of Kululu, north-east of Kayseri, might have been this capital city.[44]

The Paeonians/proto-Armenians appear to have started to settle in Tabal as from the 12th century BC and grown to a sizeable population by the 9th, when they were able to found a kingdom in the second half of that century. From this period we know the names of the first two kings, Tuatte and Kikki, whom scholars claim to be father and son.[45]

With the arrival of the Pelagonian Paeonians by the end of the 9th century BC the population of Tabal, where these migrants settled, grew considerably, enabling the following kings, Tuwatis and Wasusaramimasa, to claim the title of great king — this matter is reflected in the genealogy of Khorenatsi's prehistory of the Armenians.

The plague of around 770 BC, which had claimed the life of the king of Carchemish, Astiruwa, must also have spread to Tabal. We know from the Kululu I inscription that the king, Tuwatis, died in such a plague at around the same time as Astiruwa. The death of Tuwatis had created the opportunity for Wasusaramimasa to usurp power and become the next great king of Tabal.

So far, I have found six long inscriptions from the various parts of Tabal; these will all be fully translated in the accompanying volume. Of these inscriptions two are connected with Tuwatis (Kululu I) and Wasusaramimasa (Topada), which will be discussed under the names of these two kings.

In view of the large number of names deriving from various minor city-states, I am presenting in this section only the nine kings and one prime minister, who had overall control of the lands of Tabal. The minor kingdoms will be discussed in the next section.

Ruler	Date	Attested by
Tuatte	837; 836	Shalmaneser III; for Argishti, see below
Kikki	837; 836	Shalmaneser III
Tuwatis	770?	Kululu I; Topada
Wasusaramimasa	742; 738; 730?	Tiglath-Pileser III; Topada; Sultanhan stele
Khully	730?; 713	Tiglath-Pileser III; Sargon II
Ambaris	713	Sargon II
Ishkallu	675	Esarhaddon
Mugallu	675; 668	Esarhaddon; Ashurbanipal
...ussi	640?	Ashurbanipal
Ruwas	770?	Kululu I

Tuatte

This name is pronounced Tuwate, which means that the unwritten 'w/v' phoneme is a part of the word. The name means 'capable crown/king' ('tuw' > 't'ag' = 'crown/king' + 'at' = 'capable', as seen in the name of Khelaru*ata*). Khorenatsi's prehistory does not record this name. Tuatte is the first king of Tabal we know of through the inscription of Shalmaneser III, who in 837 and 836 BC was the first Assyrian king to venture a Tabalian campaign when Tuatte and his son Kikki together with some 20 minor kings of Tabal district capitulated and paid the tribute demanded by the Assyrians.

Kikki

This name is not explainable in the Armenian language. The Armenian onomastica records similar names, such as Giga (AD 607), Gigan (6th century AD) and Gigi (AD 1251),[46] which are also unexplainable. Kikki is the Assyrian rendering of the name, which means that we do not know how the proto-Armenian version was written or pronounced. However, the name has been correctly transcribed as Sisak ('sis' + 'ak' suffix), which is still unexplainable.

In my opinion, this name derives from the Greek Κίκυς ('strength, vigour') or Γίγας ('giant'), which is quite possible since many of the Pelagonian migrants, as discussed above, did have Greek names. It is also possible that the Sisak version of the name was in use while Kikki was in power (Assyrians record only demotic names), and that the city name of Sis or Sissu (present Kozan) derives from his name, as does that of the later grand dukedom of Sisakeans on the eastern highlands of Armenia.

Khorenatsi, in Book 1.12, records the name of Sisak and the dukedom of Sisakan, founded by the descendants of Sisak. Khorenatsi also tells us that his information comes from Mar Aba Kadina, who in this particular case could probably not have gleaned the name from the Assyrian or Babylonian inscriptions nor from the history of Berossus, since otherwise he would also, doubtless, have had mentioned the name of Tuatte, given that the two names, Tuatte and Kikki, appear together in Shalmaneser's inscription. It would seem therefore that Mar Aba's source in this case is none other than the name of the Sisakan dukedom, which will be duscussed in Part III.

Some scholars have tried to equate the names of Kikki and Kiaki, which, I find unconvincing based, as it must be, only on phonetic similarity.

Tuwatis

This name means 'storm-like crown/king' ('tuw' > 't'ag' = 'crown', 'king' + 'atis' > 'ayis' = 'wind, gale' — we have seen this word above in the name of Panamuw*atis*). His recomposed name was Aramayis meaning 'storm of Aram' ('Aram' = 'country of Aram' + 'ayis' = 'wind, gale'). In Khorenatsi's biblicised account of the progeny of Hayk, Aramayis was the one who engendered the long line of kings, which must have been due to his seniority within the kings of Aram. He used the epithet 'great king' which in proto-Armenian, as well as in the modern language, was 'apawa' > 'awaga' = 'senior, grand' (we note the word 'apawa' in Kululu I, line 6a as 'apawa mu' = 'my senior'). Aramayis may be a composition much older than the other names, because the 'ayis' ('wind, breeze, gale') part of the name belongs to periods before Classical Armenian in which the 'i' became lost, the word becoming 'ays'.

The Assyrians do not mention Tuwatis, as at his time and until the succession of Tiglath-Pileser III, Assyria was in decline. But Argishti I of Urartu, in his fourth year (783 or 777 BC) had attacked Khelaruada's Melid and on that occasion he boasts of having subjugated the "Lands of Tuatte" along with the city of Melid. Argishti's empty talk about subjugating Tabal is useful in attesting that Tuwatis was alive during his time, even though the name is wrongly spelled; unless Argishti is referring to the old king Tuatte and his dynasty, in which case he will be confirming that Tuwatis belonged to that dynasty.

I have not seen any inscription of Tuwatis, but his adviser, a certain Ruwas, has an eulogy executed on the occasion of the death of this king in the plague, which had also devastated Carchemish and claimed the life of the king, Astiruwa. Ruwas mentions the plague in the first line of Kululu I, in the sentence "awa na-ia HOUSE-na a-sa hi zi-i a-sata hatama wa ta" = "now his house left without an overseer because of the disease came to an end." It has been claimed that Tuwatis was the father of Wasusaramimasa.[47] Tuwatis had many sons, but Wasusaramimasa was not one of them. The proof of this can be seen in the following inscriptions:

> Kululu I.6a: "sati tara una ti za-ia pawa HOUSE-na zi ti" = "The vacant throne ceased to belong to his House forever."
> Sultanhan stele, line 1: "awa za na GOD THUNDER-hu i-na tu wara sasa i-na tanu waha" = "To him (Wasusaramimasa) god Tark gave guidance and secured the throne."
> Topada, line 1: "Tuwatisa GREAT KING ÁU 'INFANT' TUWA li sa" = "Tuwatis the great valiant king had many sons." "Wasusaramimasa wa STRONG ziti PAR-na ARA wasa ta" = "Wasusaramimasa came with strong men and took over the kingdom."

Hopefully, these quotations will set the record straight and rectify the misunderstanding

Wasusaramimasa
The Assyrians write this name as Uassurme. Scholars on the whole write it as Wasusarmas; but all the hieroglyphic inscriptions that contain the name show it as Wasusaramimasa. It appears that the Wasusarmas version is somewhere between the Assyrian and proto-Armenian rendering of the actual name; in other words, it is a scholarly creation, a misreading to be ignored.

The name means 'kingdom belonging to (the god) Sarami' ('wasu' > 'gaho' = 'kingdom' + 'Sarami' = the indigenous name of god Sar(ru)ma + 'masa' = 'part, share, portion'). The Classical Armenian name of this king, in Khorenatsi Book I.12, was just Harma, which is the transcription of the Hittite[?] version of the god's name Sarma. The people of the inscriptions, the proto-Armenians, called this god Sarami, which can be seen in the Topada inscription, wherein the gods are frequently invoked, and on each occasion this particular god is called Sarami.

In my earlier reference to Tuwatis, I showed that Wasusaramimasa was not one of his sons, but a usurper. All the same, that did not stop him continuing to style himself the great king, as Tuwatis had done. Khorenatsi acknowledges the importance of Harma (Wasusaramimasa) by calling him the father of Aram; in other words, the most senior king or the leading king among the kings of Aram (south-eastern Anatolia).

Wasusaramimasa was a contemporary of Tiglath-Pileser III of Assyria and of the proto-Armenian kings Sulumal of Melid, Kushtashpi of Kummukh, Kamana and Pisiris of Carchemish, Tarkulara of Gurgum, Urballa of Tukhana, Urimme of Khubishna, Ushkhitti of Tuna and Tukhamme of Ishtunda. In the third year of Tiglath-Pileser, together with the other proto-Armenian kings Wasusaramimasa paid tribute to the Assyrian while he was in Syria. He is also mentioned as tributary king in the year 732 BC.[48] After this last date it appears that he lapsed from his obligations, and Tiglath-Pileser sent his official, Rab-Shaku, who dethroned him. His replacement was a certain Khully, who could apparently satisfy the Assyrian greed for gold, silver and horses. The date of the dethronement is not known, but it must have been sometime between 732 and 729 BC.

Wasusaramimasa has left a long and difficult inscription known as the Topada inscription, of which only a part has survived. Although the end of this inscription is missing, what has survived is very important, because it is one of very few inscriptions which describes a full-blown war between Wasusaramimasa and the king of the city of Parzuta. It appears the city of Parzuta belonged to the Kaska people, who were the first to attack, under the leadership of their "courageous and mighty" king Bar-ga'ya of KTK (the 'KTK' according to Diakonoff is the Aramaean of Kaska and stands for Katak). A few scholars have tried to translate the Topada inscription. The result of such partial translatations and the attempt to translate the whole inscription remain unsatisfactory, particularly since Kiyakiya is shown as one of Wasusaramimasa's allies in his battle with Bar-ga'ya of the

Parzutean Kaska. Kiyakiya is also known as Kiakki. This king of Shinukhtu was not a contemporary of Wasusaramimasa, but belonged to the era of Sargon II (722-705 BC).

Khorenatsi, in his prehistory of the Armenians, mentions the war against the Kaska people. He names the king, Barga'ya, as Payapis K'ałya, but is unable to find which of the proto-Armenian kings was involved, which forces him to ascribe the whole affair to Aram (Book I.14), the name of the country of south-eastern Anatolia, except that he presents this Aram in the biblical style as a person, a patriarch. He mentions his source as Mar Aba Kadina, which makes one wonder how this Syriac scholar had managed to learn of this story.

Khully

This name means a 'ram' ('Aries') or 'battering-ram' ('khul-ly' > 'χoy'). The word 'χoy' is still used in modern Armenian. Khorenatsi records the name, in Book I.19, as Hoy, which is correct, as the same word has been spelled both as 'χoy' and 'hoy'.[49]

When Tiglath-Pileser III dethroned Wasusaramimasa, Khully was his choice as a client king, and yet the Assyrian tries his best to lower the dignity of his choice by adding "the son of nobody"; in other words Khully had no aristocratic pedigree. However, he must have been wealthy enough to satisfy Rab-Shaku's demands for gold (10 talents), silver (1,000 talents) and 2,000 horses.[50]

Besides Tiglath-Pileser, Khully was the contemporary of Shalmaneser V and Sargon II. According to Sargon a prince before his own time, implying Shalmaneser V, had dethroned Khully, but he himself had reinstated him in 713 BC (the ninth year of his reign) as king of the reorganized Tabal under the new name of Bit-Burutish.[51]

The date of Khully's reinstatement as king of Bit-Burutish appears to be suspect, because after Khully, his son Ambaris who should have succeeded him, and had been given Sargon's daughter in marriage, with the lands of Khilakku as dowry. But in that same year Ambaris is supposed to be negotiating with Phrygia and Urartu, for which he is dethroned and exiled to Assyria together with his entire entourage — a somewhat implausibly eventful year.

Ambaris

This name means 'grossly pompous' ('am' = 'whole, gross, entire, all' + 'bar' > 'p'ar' = 'pomp, splendour, glory, fame'). The recomposed Classical Armenian name of this prince, in Khorenatsi Book I.19, was P'arnak, meaning 'source of pomp' ('p'ar' is the same as in the proto-Armenian name + 'ak' = source).

Ambaris was the son of Khully and a favourite of Sargon II of Assyria, who gave him his own daughter, Akhat-abisha in marriage and presented him with the lands of Khilakku as dowry.[52] Ambaris was soon in diplomatic discussions with Mita of Phrygia and Rusa of Urartu, presumably, in order to avoid the heavy tribute imposed on him by his father-in-law. This state of affairs was against Assyrian interests, which forced Sargon to strike, apprehend Ambaris and exile him together with his entire entourage to Assyria. Sargon says that all these events took place in his ninth year (713 BC) of reign, which, as mentioned before, is a suspect date. But, it is also possible that Ambaris, before succeeding his father Khully, had already married Akhat-abisha and was ruling Khilakku, only taking control of Bit-Burutish after the death of his father in 713 BC. However, the inscriptions of Sargon do not mention such events.

After the exile of Ambaris it is most probable that his wife, Akhat-abisha, together with her major-domo, Nabu-le'i, continued to rule Bit-Burutish (Tabal), though Sargon records that he placed his own official over the country as governor.[53]

Ishkallu

This name means 'good-natured giant' ('ishka' > 'ska' (pronounced 'ĕska') = 'giant, huge' + 'allu' = 'good-natured'). Khorenatsi does not mention him, but records his son as

Skayorti = son of Ska (son of the giant), who helped Cyaxares in the destruction of Nineveh, and was, most probably, the father of Syennesis (Pačoyč), as we shall see in the next section.

We know nothing about Ishkallu. He had become the ruler of Tabal in unknown circumstances and had connections with Cilicia. He was acting together with Mugallu of Melid in an anti-Assyrian manner[54] at the time; but Ishkallu soon disappeared from the scene, under what circumstances we do not know, and Tabal passed into the hands of Mugallu, who as from this period is treated by the Assyrians as the king of Tabal.

Mugallu
We have already examined this name under the heading Melid.

...ussi
This name, too, has been examined under the Melid heading above.

Ruwas
This name cannot be explained in the Armenian language. Most probably the bearer of the name was a proto-Armenian with a Greek name, which is not out of the ordinary, as many of the Pelagonian Paeonian migrants at the end of the 9th century BC may have had such names. No indigenous word or name in the Armenian language starts with the 'r' phoneme.

Ruwas, as he himself testifies, was the adviser of Tuwatis, the great king of Tabal. He has left an inscription known as Kululu I, which was executed on the occasion of the death of Tuwatis. The said inscription is one of the finest from Tabal and easy to understand because of its simplicity. It tells us how Tuwatis died and what arrangements had been made for him, and how people came forth, in their Sunday best, to see the funeral. At one point he says: "Tuwatis had greatness, I wish I had died instead of him."

CHAPTER 9

MINOR KINGDOMS OF TABAL

Tabal Districts

The extensive lands of Tabal had many minor kingdoms, particularly, around Kayseri and to the west of it. It appears, every village or small city had its king, who was accountable to the central power, the great king of Tabal, and in the absence of such a king, to the Assyrian governor (the Bolkarmaden [Bulgarmaden] inscription XXXII highlights the role of the Assyrian governor). The list of kings detailed below shows that there was only one minor king mentioned in the 9th century BC and all the other names are those belonging to kings of various places of the 8th century and onwards. This means that these minor kingdoms were mostly initiated after the arrival of the Pelagonian Paeonians, who settled to the east of the Phrygians. It was this large number of minor kings that enabled the chief ruler of Tabal of the 8th century BC, such as Tuwatis and Wasusaramimasa, to use the title of 'great' king.

Of course, we know only a small proportion of these kings either through the Assyrian records or through their indigenous inscriptions, which survived to our own time.

For instance, Shalmaneser III mentions Tuatte and Kikki and twenty kings of Tabal. Of these twenty kings he records only one, Pukhamme. As for the indigenous inscriptions, these are mostly damaged, with a few in fairly good condition but in some cases lacking the name of the author; such as the long inscription of the Sultanhan stele, which lacks both the author's and his father's names.

The Armenian prehistory of Khorenatsi, in Book 1.19, mentions only five names of minor kings of Tabal from the known multitude. These five names are those of the better known ones. Of course, his information derives from the Assyrian sources.

Ruler	Date	Attested by
Pukhamme of Khubishna	837	Shalmaneser III
Urballa of Tukhana, also known as Warapalawa	742; 732	Tiglath-Pileser III; Sargon II. Inscriptions Bolkarmaden XXXII; Ivriz; Bor; Andaval.
Urimme of Khubishna	742	Tiglath-Pileser III
Ushkhitti of Atuna	742; 732	Tiglath-Pileser III
Tukhamme of Ishtunda	742; 732	Tiglath-Pileser III
Kiakki of Shinukhtu	718	Sargon II
Kurti of Atuna	718	Sargon II
Hurakhara	After 710?	Inscription Porsuk
Panuna	After 710	Inscription Kululu II
Tarkhuna	After 710	Inscription Bolkarmaden XXXII
Sapi of Karaburna	?	Inscription Karaburna XLVI
Gurti of Til-Garimmu	695	Sennacherib

Pukhamme

This name transcribes as Hoghami, which means 'carer of all' ('pukh' > 'hog' + 'hamme' > 'hami' = 'all, everyone and everything').

Shalmaneser III of Assyria mentions Pukhamme of Khubishna[55] in 837 BC, when he was campaigning in Tabal. Beside the name we know nothing about him.

Urballa

This king of Tukhana (Tuwana, the later Tyana) was the best known of all the minor kings and was commemorated in many inscriptions, of which two at Ereğli, known as the Bor and the Ivriz inscriptions, were his own creations. He was a vassal of Wasusaramimasa, the great king, as his name suggests. He too had his own subordinates of even smaller kingdoms. His indigenous name was Warapalawa, but the Assyrians record only the demotic Urballa. Significantly, the two names, Warapalawa and Urballa, do not correlate.

Urballa means 'good satellite' ('urb' = 'satellite' + 'al' = 'salt', a term of endearment, having the sense of 'good old boy' or a flattering, caressing and diminutive suffix as seen in the name of Sulum*al*).

Warapalawa means 'one who conducts good conversation' or 'one who puts up a good fight', because the 'pa' stem can mean both 'to talk' and 'to fight' (also 'smoke'). The analysis is: 'wara' = 'to conduct, to drive' + 'pa' = 'talk, fight' + 'lawa' = 'good' ('wara' should not be confused with the other 'wara', meaning 'to burn, fire, blaze').

Khorenatsi in Book 1.19 mentions the name of this king as Arbak, which means 'good satellite' ('arb' = 'urb', 'satellite', having the sense of 'vassal' and 'subordinate', + 'ak', an endearing suffix which has replaced the proto-Armenian 'al'). According to Khorenatsi, who does not know the indigenous name Warapalawa, the name derives from the Assyrian records.

Warapalawa (Urballa) had a long reign and had been a contemporary of Tiglath-Pileser, Shalmaneser V and Sargon of Assyria — he must have been a smooth operator and a master of persuasion. Being subordinate to Wasusaramimasa, the great king of Tabal, it is possible that he had contributed fighting men for the war against the Parzuteans.

His name appears, as a tributary, in years 742 and 732 BC in Tiglath-Pileser's inscription.

The last mention of his name falls in 710 BC when he had

sent a message to the Assyrian governor, Ashur-shara-usur, concerning an attack by the people of Ishtunda and Atuna on Bit-Burutish.[56]

Urimme

This is the Assyrian rendering of the name. We do not have the indigenous version of it. Hawkins writes this name as U(i)rimme, which, if correct, can be explained as 'what a loftiness' ('uir' > 'ger' = 'high, higher, elevated' + 'ime' = 'what a' — a preposition).

Khorenatsi mentions this name, in Book 1.19, as Perč, which means 'elegant, sumptuous, magnificent, superb, etc'.

He is mentioned by Tiglath-Pileser III as a tributary in 742 BC. Urimme may have been another subordinate of Wasusaramimasa who contributed fighting men to the war against the Parzuteans.

Ushkhitti

Again, this is the Assyrian rendering of the name, which in this case makes good sense even in the modern Armenian language. Ushkhitti means 'the time of the highly intelligent' ('ush' = 'mind, memory, intelligence, wise' + 'khit' = 'condensed, concentrated, compact' + 'ti' = 'time, period'). Khorenatsi does not mention this name.

Tiglath-Pileser acknowledges him as a tributary in the years 742 and 732 BC.

Ushkhitti was the ruler of Atuna (Tuna), which means he was a subordinate to Wasusaramimasa and, therefore, should have contributed fighting men to the war against the Parzuteans.

Tukhamme

He was the ruler of Ishtunda, mentioned by Tiglath-Pileser as a tributary in the years 742 and 732 BC. The geographical position of Ishtunda is not yet known, but it must have been near to Warapalawa's Tukhana and Ushkhitti's Atuna, which means that he too, as a subordinate, must have contributed fighting men to Wasusaramimasa's war against the Parzuteans.

Tukhamme means 'resists all' ('tuk' > 'tok' = 'resist, persist, endure' + 'hame' = 'all, everything and everyone'). Khorenatsi does not mention this name.

Kiakki

This is the Assyrian version of the name. His indigenous name was Kiyakiya(?),[57] the reduplicated form of Kia, minus the ak suffix, which makes sense, and would confirm my explanation of the name. Unfortunately, I have found no evidence to support the Kiyakiya reading. In the Topada inscription of Wasusaramimasa the Kiyakiya and Warapalawa names do not appear.

The part of the inscription, which is supposed to mention these two names has been misunderstood. It reads: "EARTH sa ta wara pana wasu 241-ia 241-ia sa haru sa ta" = (the king of Parzuta attacked me because I did not exalt him as a great king) "created havoc, and opened the kingdom's STABLES. He smashed the STABLES (and fording the river disappeared across my borders with a great number of horses, which he kept)." I have not yet seen the Aksaray stele nor the Kululu lead strips (No.1), therefore cannot at present make any further comments in this connection.

The name Kiakki means 'source of life' ('kia' > 'kea' = 'life' + 'ak' = 'source'); the name Kiyakiya means "life! life!" ('kea kea'). In Khorenatsi's prehistory, Book 1.19, the name of this ruler is mentioned as Głak, which means 'source of intense desire'. The 'gł' of Głak is the word 'gełj' (the final 'j' is an augmentative suffix pronounced 'dz'); the actual stem is 'geł', which in the formation of the compound has lost the un-accented 'e' vowel, because the accent of the name falls on the last syllable of the 'ak' stem = 'source'. (Note that the Classical Armenian era compounds keep the augmentative suffix 'j', which means this name must have been composed prior to the said times.)

Kiakki is mentioned only in 718 BC by Sargon II as one who did not send tribute and was dethroned and taken to Assyria; his kingdom being placed under an Assyrian governor, a proto-Armenian eunuch by the name of Kurti, as we will see below. Therefore, Kiakki could not have been a contemporary of Wasusaramimasa and he could not have participated in the war against the Parzuteans, which must have taken place sometime around the middle of the eighth century BC.

Lukenbill's translation of the part where Kiakki is involved, and his unwillingness to send tribute reads: "Kiakki of the city of Shinukhtu forgot the oath; decided not to pay tribute", which had rightly prompted the reasoning that one can forget only an existing oath; therefore, in the past, before Sargon's time, Kiakki must have agreed to pay a certain amount of tribute to the Assyrians. However, the same part of Sargon's inscription, as translated by A. G. Lie, is slightly different, and reads: "Kiakki of Shinukhtu ignored the decision of the great gods, and in order to withhold his tribute he became negligent towards me." The implications of this second translation are different; it can mean that in Sargon's time it was decided that a certain amount of tribute should be paid by Kiakki.

Kurti

This is a demotic name and a not flattering one at that. The meaning of the name suggests to me that the bearer was a eunuch. Such persons were rather favoured by the Assyrians and there are other examples of this; such as Kulani of Kinalua and Kirri of Que, as we will see below.

Kurti means 'the time of the shameful', which has its exact recomposition in Khorenatsi, in Book 1.19, as Korak. Kur of Kurti and Kor of Korak are the same word and both mean 'shameful, of head bowed (in shame), crooked, etc'. The 'ti' of the first name means 'time' and the 'ak' of the latter is a diminutive suffix.

Kurti was a contemporary both of Tiglath-Pileser and Sargon, who after removing Kiakki from Shinukhtu entrusted the governorship of the city to Kurti of Atuna.

Hurakhara

He is the author of the Porsuk inscription (Meriggi No. 29) and the son of Atis ('wind'). He also gives the name of his ancestor as Hurnasa, which means 'the fiery'. I do not know to what date he belongs, but the inscription and the palaeography are similar to the BOR inscription.

The name Hurakhara means 'blaze of fire' ('hura' = 'of fire', in the genitive + 'χara' = 'blaze, burn'). His father's name was Atis, according to the inscription, which means 'wind', as we have seen in the names of Tuwatis and Panamuwatis. We know nothing about this minor ruler and Khorenatsi does not mention him in his prehistory.

Panuna

We know this name through his own inscription of Kululu II. The said inscription comes from a time when Tabal was an Assyrian governorship, therefore, it can be dated to 709 BC or after. The matter of the governorship is obvious, even though the inscription does not mention it in so many words. No other name is mentioned in this inscription, not even that of his father. It is all about how badly he had been treated for the kindness he had shown to another unnamed person.

Tarkhuna

This name, too, derives from his own inscription Bolkarmaden XXXII. He says that he was the son of Tarkhuwara; an adviser of Warapalawa.

Tarkhuna means 'Tark the successful' ('tark' = 'thunder' + 'huna' = 'to succeed, to prosper, to ford [a river] and a ford') — this 'huna' stem we see in Carchemish A 6.5 as 'puna' in "BAR tara puna sa" = "he succeeded to the throne." The father's name means 'Tark the charger' ('tark' = 'thunder' + 'hu' = 'to charge, attack, group, horde' + 'wara' = 'to conduct', as in the name of Warapalawa). Both names are absent from Khorenatsi's pre-history.

The inscription says: "Warapalawa gave me advancement, his great kingdom came to me by the help of the all seeing god, but a certain Mutina tried to take over by trickery. The great judge came to adjudicate [this would be the Assyrian governor whose flag is illustrated] and decided in my favour." The contents of the inscription place it in the period after 709 BC and raise some doubts about a son and successor of Warapalawa, with the name of Muwahara.

Sapi

Nothing is known of this minor ruler, who has left one of the most difficult inscriptions in Karaburna. The inscription has its beginning, parts of its lines, and its end, missing, which makes the translation extremely difficult. The language is provincial but marks the beginnings of the later word developments; such as 'sama', which other inscriptions use to denote 'all, everything, totality, etc'. In this inscription it means 'pleasing', and for 'all, everything, totality' it uses the word 'hama'; the word 'zati', which others use to denote 'separate, share, part and choosing', he uses in this inscription for the sense of 'himself' or 'personally'.

The sense of the inscription is that a fortress was left to him by his forefathers. Sapi, after his accession, goes travelling in order to view his state. He sees the fortress, which he admires, but is not delighted, because it is under someone else's rule, therefore, Sapi fights in order to take possession. I do not find a "Sipis and his Nis's son making samanza" in this inscription, as it has been claimed by another translator. The 'na-ia' ('to view') has been made into 'niyas' and 'sama za' ('pleased with it') has been made into 'samanza' (with no knowledge what this word means).

The name Sapi means 'valorous feat' ('sapi' > 'haw-i' = 'valorous feat, victory, triumph').

The date of this inscription is not known, but judging from the language used it must belong to the seventh century BC.

Gurdi

This name belongs to Til-Garimmu (House of T'orgom), which city was on the eastern border of Tabal. The name is the Assyrian rendering and means 'time of the rebel/insurgent' ('gur' = 'rebel, insurgent, to snarl' + 'ti' = 'time, period'). The Classical Armenian recomposition of the name, in Khorenatsi Book 1.19, which derives from the Assyrian sources, was Gorak, of which the initial syllable 'gor' is the same as the 'gur' of Gurti, but the 'ti' ending of the proto-Armenian name has been changed to the word 'ak', which means 'source'; therefore, the Classical Armenian name means 'a person who is the source of rebellion', which is a perfect match.

The name Gurdi (previously read as Hidi) appears in Sennacherib's inscription, which describes in a few words the campaign against Til-Garimmu in 695 BC. Sennacherib says that a certain Gurdi "had consolidated the kingdom" and had rebelled against Assyria. With the help of the gods, earthwork and siege engines Sennacherib's general managed to capture the city but Gurdi had escaped, as there is no further mention of his name.

A stela has been found in Karahüyük near Elbistan, which was in the district of Til-Garimmu. The inscription of this stela has been translated, but the translation and the contents of the inscription are two different things. Furthermore, the time of the raising of this stela has been ascribed to the wrong period. It belongs to 695 BC, to the time of the Assyrian attacks, and describes in detail the treatment of the population and the hardship at the hands of the assailants. The author does not divulge his name, but tells us that the king of Assyria, naming him "Moon made wish come true" (Sin Ahhe Eriba, popularly known as Sennacherib), was ill with fever and sent his men to punish the country. By the time the attacks ceased, he says, there was not enough food even for a mouse to subsist.

CHAPTER 10

THE VARIOUS KINGDOMS OF CILICIA

The end of Kizzuwatna

The Hittites, starting with the 16th century BC, called this country Kizzuwatna, known to the Egyptians as Kode. Kizzuwatna had been a strong unified Hurrian kingdom, but the 12th century population upheavals known as the Sea Peoples movement had put an end to the kingdom and the name of Kizzuwatna. It appears that during this period some Mycenaeans had settled in the eastern plains of the country, which the Assyrians called Que and later the Romans named Cilicia Campestris; the mountainous western regions of the country became known as Cilicia Aspera or Tracheia.

The proto-Armenians who had arrived in Anatolia as the Paeonian people, appear to have shunned Cilicia until the beginning of the 9th century BC. It must also be admitted that from the middle of the 12th century BC to the beginning of the 9th, Cilicia does not loom large in history. It is only in the course of the 9th century that a reinvigorated Assyria with expantionist ambitions under Shalmaneser III, brings the country to historical notice as Que, Khilakku and so on.

During the Middle Ages this whole region of southern Anatolia became known to the Armenians as Kilikia (Cilicia), where, starting from the last decade of the 11th century AD, the independent Armenian kingdom of Cilicia was established, which lasted until AD 1375.

The proto-Armenian rulers of Cilicia start appearing in the Assyrian records in the time of Shalmaneser III, that is by the middle of the 9th century BC. However, instead of a unified country, as Kizzuwatna was, there sprang up new city states of transient duration, continuing well into the 6th century BC, and a strong unified Cilicia emerged only after Syennesis, at a time when there were no other independent proto-Armenian rulerships.

Cilicia, as a whole, has produced no hieroglyphic inscriptions — or at least no such inscriptions have been found, except for one, which belongs to Azatiwata (Norayr), and was discovered in 1946 at the mound of Karatepe, to the north-east of Adana. Azatiwata's inscription is a unique document, the longest of its type with a Phoenician translation. Unfortunately, the hieroglyphic version and the Phoenician translation are not identical. This will be discussed under the name of Azatiwata below.

This inscription attests Azatiwata, though his name is not recorded by the Assyrians, whereas all the other names given below derive from Assyro-Babylonian sources.

Khorenatsi in Book 1.22 of his prehistory gives us his third and last name-list of the proto-Armenian rulers. This third list is the most orderly of all the name-lists and the names are those of the Cilician rulers. Khorenatsi says that Mar Aba had gleaned these names from the history of Abydenus. This list quotes nine kings, of which the first one is the result of a misunderstanding, and the last two are those of Median governors (these last two names are mentioned in the 'Cyropaedia' of Xenophon [book III] as kings of Armenia).

In the next chapter the misunderstood first name just mentioned, which is so important for Armenian prehistory, will be discussed, and it will also be shown why the proto-Armenians of Cilicia, like the proto-Armenians of Kummukh, did not participate in the migration to the Urartian highlands, whereas the bulk of the population of the other kingdoms did. This misunderstood name may also clarify the disappearance of Ishkallu of Tabal (discussed in Chapter 8 above) and the fate of his son, who, at a time when there were no more proto-Armenian rulers, emerges as the first new ruler of Cilicia Campestris.

Ruler	Date	Attested by
Pikhirim of Kilakku	858	Shalmaneser III
Kate of Que	858; 839; 834/3	Shalmaneser III
Kirri of Que	833	Shalmaneser III
Tulli of Tanakun	834/3	Shalmaneser III
Azatiwata of Adana	760?	His own inscription of Karatepe
Kirua of Illubru	696/5	Sennacherib
Sanduarri of Sissu & Kundu	769-676	Esarhaddon
Sandasarme of Khilakku	668	Ashurbanipal
Syennesis of Cilicia	585	Herodotus 1:74
Appuwashu of Pirindu	557	Neriglisar

Pikhirim

The explanation of this name is 'rebellious, for which (he is) admired' or 'admired for his insurgency' ('pi' > 'hi' = 'admire, revere, exhalt' + 'khir' > 'kher' = 'insurgent, rebel' + 'im' = 'for what, how') which in the Classical Armenian era has been recomposed as 'P'arnawaz' (Khorenatsi, Book 1.22). P'arnawaz has the sense of 'famous for his fiery nature' ('p'arn' = 'fame, glory' + 'aw' = 'being, essence' + 'az' = 'fire' — as in the name Tarkun*az*i).

Others have explained this name differently; for instance Hübschmann interprets it as 'magnificent arm', and compares it with the Iranian Parnabuzu; in other words, he suggests that the name is a loan from the Iranian. His explanation suffers from two errors. Firstly he fails to note that the Armenian name is written P'arna*w*az, with a 'w' and not 'b'; secondly, the explanation creates an article 'a' or a conjunction 'a' between 'p'arn' and 'waz' (if we are to accept that 'waz' = 'baz'). The ancient compounds do not contain such an article or conjunction, as illustrated throughout this study. P'arnawaz is of indigenous Armenian composition, and the phonetic resemblance with the Iranian name is accidental. We note also the 'awaz' ending of the name in Man*awaz* of Gurgum (see above page 85).

Pikhirim was a contemporary of Shalmaneser III of Assyria, who in 858 BC attacked Unqi (Patin) where he faced the Syro-Hittite alliance comprising Sam'al, Bit-Adini, Carchemish, Unqi, Que and Khilakku of Pikhirim.

Kate

The name means 'the durable' ('kate' > 'kay' = 'there is, exists, station, persist, condition'). This name does not appear in Khorenatsi's history.

Kate is attested by Shalmaneser III of Assyria, as he was one of the members of the Syro-Hittite alliance at the battle of Unqi (Patin). In 839 Shalmaneser attacked Kate's Que, and plundered the cities of Lusanda, Abarnani and Kisnanti. This was repeated by the Assyrians in 834, but this time the plundered cities were Timur, Tarzu (Tarsus) and Pakhri (the Armenian Par — see this name under Cilicia in Part III [page 183] and note 19).

In 833 Shalmaneser replaced Kate with his brother Kirri as the ruler of Que, though nothing is said of the fate of Kate on this replacement. Considering the efforts of the Assyrians to contain Kate throughout his rulership, it is amazing how long he lasted. Perhaps, it was this remarkable durability that earned him the name of Kate.

Kirri

He was the brother of Kate, replacing him in 833 BC as ruler of Que at the instance of Shalmaneser. His name suggests that he was effeminate or even a eunuch. Kirri means 'the lewd' or 'the effeminate' ('kir' > 'sir' = 'lewd, effeminate, debaucher, womanish, loose, etc'). Khorenatsi does not mention this name.

Tulli

He was a minor ruler in Tanakun, which remains a geographically unknown place in Cilicia. All of our information about him comes from Shalmaneser's inscription, which says, in referring to Kate, that the city of Tanakun of Tulli was also plundered in 834/3 BC.

Tulli means 'the forgiver' ('tul' > 't'oł' = 'forgive, to let go'). He is not mentioned by Khorenatsi in his prehistory.

Azatiwata

This name means 'blazing dawn' ('az' = 'fire, blaze' + 'atiw' > 'ayig' > 'ayg' = 'dawn, morning' + 'ta' = 'he' — the connotation is 'a man of new times'). Azatiwata also calls himself Asizatiwara, which means 'the chosen fire' ('asi' = 'different' + 'zati' = 'choice' + 'wara' = 'fire') and Asizatiwata 'the chosen'. He built a fortress city which was named Asizatiwaya in his honour — the 'ta' ending of the previous two names having been replaced by the toponymic suffix 'ya'. Khorenatsi, in his prehistory, Book 1.19, records this name as Norayr, which means 'new fire' ('nor' = 'new' + 'ayr' = 'fire'). The modern sense of this name is 'new man' which betrays the influence of the Greek name 'Neandros'.

Azatiwata's inscription is essentially the celebration of one person and his deeds It involves no other state and none is mentioned. Beside his own name, Azatiwata, there are only two more, Awarakusa and the 'House of Mukasa'. As for cities, he mentions only Adana, the seat of government, Pahara, and the fortress city Asizatiwaya. that he himself had built.

Expert opinion usually identifies the name of Awarakusa of the text, with Urikki of the Assyrian inscriptions. According to the Karatepe inscription, such an equivalance is not workable.

Urikki was attested by Tiglath-Pileser III as a tributary in the year 738 BC. In 715 BC, Sargon II put an end to Urikki's rulership and the country became an Assyrian province under the governorship of Ashur-shara-usur. Under these circumstances Azatiwata could not belong to this period, because, there was no son or successor of Urikki "to raise to his father's throne" (sentence XVI). It is inconceivable that the Assyrians would have let Azatiwata to build his fortress within the period starting with Tiglath-Pileser to the early years of Ashurbanipal — the last Assyrian governorship is attested for the year 655 BC.

Azatiwata writes that he was an adviser ('miti') of Awarakusa (sentence I), and on the death of the latter he assumed the rulership of the kingdom, making sure that the son, after reaching a certain age (sentence XV), should succeed his father. It will be at the time of his regency that the fortress city of Asizatiwaya (Karatepe) was built. All these circumstances mean that Awarakusa and Urikki could not be the same person, but father and son, and Azatiwata's regency could not be later than 760BC when he started to build the fortress. He mentions that when the fortress was finished he was a very old man (sentence XLIX) — he refers to himself as 'sapi' = 'great-grandfather'.

It is interesting to note that Azatiwata played a similar role to Yarairaisa of Carchemish, that is, he took care of the kingdom until the time when the dead king's son was old enough to succeed to the throne. The name of Mukasa has been identified with Mopsus of the Greek tradition. There have been a few legendary persons with the name of Mopsus in Greek tradition; of these the one of Trojan fame, who travelled to Cilicia and beyond with Amphilochus and Calchas, is usually identified with Mukasa. This is because the Phoenician version of the Karatepe text mentions "Awarakusa king of DNNYM = Danunim", which sounds similar to Homer's Danaan in the *Iliad*. But this Mopsus is alleged to have died in Ascalon. Furthermore Shalmaneser III campaigned in Que in the year

858 BC, plundered the cities of Tarzu (Tarsus) and Pakhar (Pahar of Azatiwata where he says he stored barley as a pecaution against difficult times — sentence VII) in the year 834, and on both dates he records the name of the king of Que as Kate, who was replaced by his brother Kirri in 833 BC. It follows that before Awarakusa there could not have been a House of Mopsus of Adana (sentences XXI and LVIII).

There are alternative solutions to the problem of Azatiwata's House of Mukasa. It is well known that the Mycenaeans have been establishing trading settlements in eastern Mediterranean, one of which was in the Turkish Hatay,[58] reported in the Amarna letter written by Abi-milki of Tyre to Amenophis IV. Also, with the coming of the Sea People to south-eastern Anatolia, more Mycenaeans settled in Cilicia Campestris, whereas the bulk of the migrants wandered further south to the coastal Canaan, where their place of settlement became known as Palestine. It is possible that one of the Mycenaean families of Adana, bearing the name of Mukasa, had in time acquired wealth and prominence, and by the start of the 8th century BC had managed to usurp power. Alternatively, the Mopsus dynasty of Lydia, reported by Xanthus and Nicolaus Damascene,[59] under pressure from the newly-arrived Phrygians at the end of the 9th century BC, might have moved to Cilicia Campestris and there established the House of Mukasa at a time when Assyrian power was on the wane.

The Phoenician version of Azatiwata's inscription gives the sense of the sentences of the hieroglyphic text, which is full with details. The want of details in the Phoenician version makes the two variants similar but not identical. In support of this point I quote a few examples below. The sentence numbers are those of Meriggi and the Phoenician translation of the sentences derive from 'On the problems of Karatepe: the hieroglyphic text' by J. D. Hawkins and A. Morpurgo-Davies in *Anatolian Studies*, 28, 1978:

VII. For the sustenance of the people of the kingdom I stored barley in Pahar city in case of difficulties.

PHOENICIAN: and I filled the storehouses[?] of P'R.

IX. (and) trained the men of the state and furnished the state with army.

PHOENICIAN: and shield upon shield (I made).

XI. (and) purged the vainglorious persons who hardly had any nobleness.

PHOENICIAN: and I broke the proud.

LIX. If a vainglorious king from the mixture of kings, or a great person from the multitude of persons who commands a name of meaning says . . .

PHOENICIAN: If a king among kings, or a prince among princes, if a man who (is) a man of name (says) . . .

Kirua

This name means 'the passionate' ('kir-ri' > 'sir-o' = 'love, passion').

Kirua was a contemporary of Sennacherib of Assyria and the governor of Illubru in Cilicia. He was most probably a eunuch. In 696 BC he revolted and was joined by the people of Khilakku, Ingira and Tarsus. The Assyrians suppressed this revolt at a great cost to themselves. It appears that this revolt coincides with that of Gurdi of Til-Garimmu (Togarmah, the Armenian House of T'orgom).

Sanduarri

This name means 'fiery brave person' ('sand' > 'shant'/'shand' = 'thunderbolt, fire, spark' + 'u(w)' = 'person, being' + 'arri' = 'brave, courageous'). His Classical Armenian recomposed name, in Khorenatsi Book 1.19, is Arnak, which means 'source of bravery' ('arn' = 'brave, courageous' + 'ak' = 'source').

This is the second name in the list of Khorenatsi's names that is recorded twice. The first time as Arnak and the second time as Haykak, which has the same meaning as Arnak and may be his original name at birth because Arnak is a demotic name. Khorenatsi, also, has a footnote against this name which says "they say about him that he was a contemporary of Belokos (Esarhaddon?) and created a foolish commotion wherein he died".

Sanduarri was ruler of Kundu (Anavarza, the Armenian Anabazar) and Sissu (present-day Kozan — the capital city Sis of the Cilician kingdom of 11th to 14th century AD) and a contemporary of Esarhaddon of Assyria. In 679 BC he sealed an anti-Assyrian alliance with Abdi-Milkutti of Sidon, but was soon overcome and together with his ally was captured and beheaded in 676 BC.[60]

Sandasarme

This name means 'the fiery look of the moon' ('sand' = 'thunderbolt, fire, spark' + 'aš' = 'to look, to view' — the verb is 'ashel' + 'arme' = 'the moon'). The Classical Armenian recomposed name, in Khorenatsi Book 1.22, is Hratchia, which means 'fiery eyes' ('hr' > 'hur' = fire, blaze + atchk' = 'eyes' – 'atchia' = 'having eyes'). The proto-Armenian name avoids using the word 'eye', which is substituted by the 'moon', as 'an eye in the sky'.

Meillet, in *Interdiction de vocabulaire* (page 16), explains this unwillingness to mention the word 'eye' as an ancient taboo, which still exists in Polynesian social custom. The same taboo is responsible for the Icelandic word 'súil', which means 'sun' but is used to denote an eye. There is, also, an example of this attitude in the inscriptions of Katuwa of Carchemish, who in A 11.3 says "GOD TARK 'nara' sa kura wa na izi" — "God Tark his eyes be blinded." 'Nara' means 'a hole, button-hole, split and ring', which is used in order to denote the eyes of a person. Therefore 'the fiery look of the moon' should be understood as 'fiery eyes'.

Sandasarme was the ruler of Khilakku and a contemporary of Ashurbanipal of Assyria, who records the receipt of an embassy from Sandasarme in the year 668 BC.[61]

Syennesis

This name means 'builder and adorner' ('syen' > 'shen' = 'building, builder, happy, populated' + 'nes-is' > 'nish' = 'ornament, example, happening'). He is mentioned by Khorenatsi, in Book 1.22, as 'Pačoyč', which means 'adorn with, ornament, embellishment, adornment'.

Syennesis was a contemporary of Nabuchadrezzar II of Babylon. At the end of the Medo-Lydian war (591-585 BC), he was one of the mediators on behalf of Cyaxares. Under his reign Cilicia prospered as an independent kingdom and at the time it was the only indigenous proto-Armenian monarchy, though subordinate to the Medians.

Syennesis's name became a dynastic name in Cilicia, since we know of others who bore that name. The development of Cilicia into a large, strong and prosperous state was due solely to the fact that the proto Armenian population, like those of Kummukh, did not move into Urartu along with the others in c. 588/87 BC.

Syennesis was the successor of Skayorti (Skayorti himself was the son of Ishkallu: 'ishka' > 'ska'; 'Skayorti' = 'son of Ska'), he might even have been a son, who had allied himself with Cyaxares at the battle for Nineveh in 612 BC and for his services was made king of Pahar (the Armenian Par, the later Misis) in Cilicia Campestris.

Appuwashu

This name means 'person of fearsome talk' ('ap' > 'ah' = 'awe, fright, horror' + 'puw' > 'hog' = 'person, soul, being' + 'ashu' = 'of talk'). His name appears in Khorenatsi's prehistory, Book 1.22, as 'P'aros', which means 'empty words' ('bar' = 'word' = 'os' = 'empty'). The Classical Armenian name has come to us in three different spellings. Various manuscripts have the name as P'aros (the critical edition), Pavos (Malkhazyants edition), and Paos (the Georgian edition). All these versions have 'P'' as the initial letter, which would render the name unexplainable. The initial letter should be 'B'. Of the three versions Baros and Baos make sense and would yield a meaning similar as the proto-Armenian name, but Bavos yields the meaning 'empty border' or 'empty kiss'.

Appuwashu was a contemporary of Neriglisar of Babylon. His domain was Pirindu, in the west of Cilicia (Cilicia Tracheia) and he prospered until he attacked various cities in Syria, which, in 557 BC, brought Neriglisar against him. Neriglisar pursued Appuwashu all the way to the Lycian borders, and the latter was not heard of again.

TWO NAMES FROM UNQI (PATINU) AND A NAME FROM HUBUSHKIA

Unqi (Patinu)

This Iron Age kingdom with its capital city Kinalua, had a long history under different names, which is not the subject of this study. Also, the two kings known as Lubarna I and II by Ashurnasirpal II and Shalmaneser III will be ignored, irrespective of the fact that their name is explainable in the Armenian language as 'lame the brave'. The prehistory of Khorenatsi records only two names belonging to Unqi and that is what will now be discussed.

Ruler	Date	Attested by
Surri	831	Shalmaneser III
Kulani	738	Tiglath-Pileser III

Surri

The name is Sur as the 'ri' ending is a suffix belonging to the Assyrian language. 'Sur' means 'a sword, sharp' and has many connotations, as in any language.

Khorenatsi mentions this Sur in Book 1.19 and has a note

against the name, which says: "Sur was a contemporary of Joshua, son of Nun". This note is chronologically correct, except for a slight interpolation due to Khorenatsi. The name Joshua in Armenian is written as Hesu. The middle 's' of Hesu is Khorenatsi's own addition. Before the discovery of the Armenian alphabet in the first decade of the fifth century the compiler or compilers of these name-lists could not have known of a Hesu, son of Nun, as Hesu is not mentioned by any source other than the Old Testament. However, these compilers would have known the name of Jehu via the Assyrian inscriptions or history. The name Jehu in Armenian is written as Heu, without the 's' of Hesu, which means that Heu, a contemporary of Surri was the king of Israel and the son of Jehoshaphat (II Kings 9).

Surri must have been the demotic name, because the 'sharp' sense of the name in hieroglyphic inscriptions is indicated by a knife (sign 336), which has been used in various inscriptions to denote 'rebellion, insurgency, brave, courageous'. Of these attributes rebellious was definitely the one applicable to Surri.

In 831 BC there was a rebellion in Kinalua and the king of Unqi, Lubarna II, was assassinated. A usurper by the name of Surri seized the throne, an event not in the interest of Assyria. Shalmaneser III sent his *turtanu* or military commander Dayyan-Ashur, to quell the insurrection. When the Assyrian army arrived at the gates of Kinalua, the inhabitants in fear of the consequences immediately surrendered up Surri and his accomplices. It is thought that Surri then committed suicide.

Kulani

This name means 'radiance without say', that is without influence in matters of state ('kul' > 'sol' > 'ts'ol' = 'shine, radiance, glow' + 'ani' = 'no say'). 'Kul' usually transcribes as 'sol', but in this case it has given as 'ts'ol'; Greek 'selas'. It is obvious from the explanation of the name that Kulani was not a ruler, but an Assyrian governor and a eunuch. His recomposed Classical Armenian name was Ts'olak, which means 'source of radiance ('ts'ol' is the 'kul' of

Kulani and means 'radiance, shine' + 'ak' = 'source').

This name appears in Khorenatsi's history, Book 1.12 under the 'progeny of Hayk', which is chronologically inexact, because Surri, who ruled before him, is recorded in the second name-list, Book 1.19. There is a good reason for this anomaly, which will be explained in chapter 15.

Tiglath-Pileser III reorganized Unqi (Patinu) in 738 BC as an Assyrian province under the governorship of the eunuch Kulani and named the country after him as Kullani.

Hubushkia (Kadmukhi)

The city of Hubushkia in Kadmukhi had a long history as a country of the Hurrians. The proto-Armenians had only one ruler in this city, whom Khorenatsi calls Kadmos, because he has not managed to find the real name of this ruler.

Khorenatsi's Kadmos has nothing to do with the Phoenician Cadmus and derives from the name of the country of Kadmukhi. In the ancient oral history of the Armenians this Kadmos is made a grandson of Hayk, the primogenitor, which, in a way, shows that for the proto-Armenians of Aram, Kadmukhi was not an important kingdom and they did not try to take possession of the country as they did in south-eastern Anatolia.

The only proto-Armenian king of Hubushkia was **Dadi**, who was a contemporary of Shamshi-Adad V. 'Dadi' means 'law, justice, logic and right'. According to Adjaryan, this name also occurs in the Iranian language. However, the meaning of the Iranian name is 'gift, tax and duty', which differs from the Armenian meaning.

Ctesias, quoted by Diodorus Siculus (Book II.1.4-8 — Loeb ed., vol. I, p. 351) mentions an Armenian king at the time of Ninus (Shamshi-Adad V), but the name quoted is Barzanes. Shamshi-Adad in his third campaign refers to the king of Hubushkia as Dadi. At the time of Shamshi-Adad, 823-811 BC, there was not such a country as Armenia, nor a people called

Armenians. For this reason, I believe Ctesias's account does not make sense, unless Dadi was also known as Barzanes, a matter of which we know nothing. We will see in the next chapter how the descendants of this king, Dadi, survived as the House of the Kadmeans to the time of the first Arsacid king of Atropatene.

PART

III

CHAPTER 12

HAYK THE PRIMOGENITOR

Patriarch of the Armenian nation
The legend of Hayk is the most striking tradition of the Armenians. Khorenatsi, fifteen centuries ago, had appreciated the importance of Hayk and had treated the story as a true historical event. He had presented Hayk as the patriarch (after the fashion of the Bible) of the Armenian nation, for which he had a very good reason, as we will see. In my opinion, his only extravagance was the biblical connection he created in order to justify his religion. But, in those days he could not have treated his story differently, because failure to adhere to the teachings of the Bible would have undermined both religion and his own standing as a bishop, which prompted him to declare that his history "will start from the same epoch as the church chroniclers do in conformity with the Christian religion". In persuit of this objective he connected Hayk to the "building of the unruly Tower of Babel", which, besides adding religious prestige, also made Hayk as old as the tower itself.

Hayk was the most important personality of proto-Armenian history, and Khorenatsi was justified in celebrating him in the extravagant manner, because Hayk was the only proto-Armenian who battled with the Assyrians and prevailed, actually slaying the Assyrian king Bel (Sargon II). Hayk's victory delivered the proto-Armenians from the yoke of the Assyrians for the first time in their history. Thus Hayk became the most famous liberating hero, the greatest proto-Armenian. Hayk became the father of the nation.

Khorenatsi had written the story of Hayk in a spirit of national pride and believed it to be a true account of the beginning of the Armenian prehistory, even though he had not understood what Hayk and his son Aramanyak, and the host of the names he had recorded actually represented. He presented in colourful language the oral history, more or less, in the manner he had managed to glean from various 'songs'.

In the Golden Age (fifth century AD) the Armenian translators of the Bible had named the Orion constellation Hayk, after their primogenitor. This means that the learned 'Fathers', the translators of the Bible, knew the story of Hayk before Khorenatsi wrote his history. It also means that they knew the meaning of the word Hayk as a 'huge Hay', a giant and a warrior. It follows that the story of Hayk must have been well known in Armenian learned circles and that Mar Aba had no role in it; he had furnished the names of the past rulers of Aram gleaned from Assyrian sources but had written nothing involving the Armenian highlands. The events and stories concerning the Armenian highlands were Khorenatsi's own contribution, which he had procured from various local oral sources and had combined them with the information contained in Mar Aba's book, which may be the reason for his mistakes, such as treating Ardashēs and Tigran the Great as Arsacids and placing them within a confused chronology.

The Armenians, up to the beginning of the fifth century AD, had not written literature, nor archives, in the Armenian language.[1] Their information about the past was to be found in the oral traditions, which do not mention any of the actual proto-Armenian names, including that of Hayk. All the names that Khorenatsi records are those recomposed in the Classical Armenian period, which have the same meanings as the more ancient proto-Armenian names. Khorenatsi does not know any of the old names including that of Hayk, which we find only in the Assyrian sources as Eshpai.

Eshpai, the powerful Hay

The proto-Armenian provenance of the name Eshpai is certain. The Assyrians had not translated the name into their own language, but had transcribed it as they had done with all the other names. It follows that the name Eshpai cannot be explained in the Assyrian language, which led western scholars to speculate that it might have belonged to the Cimmerians, even though they were unable to explain it or furnish any evidence.

Eshpai is a compound word and consists from 'esh' + 'Pai', which means 'ass Hay' ('esh' > 'ēš' + 'Pai' > 'Hay'), meaning 'a huge and powerful Hay (Armenian)'. The word 'esh' derives from the Indo-European *ekwo-, and as in any other language has the connotations of 'brave, giant, strong, stubborn, masculine, etc'.

The story of the war between Hayk and the Assyrians, known as the "battle of Hayk and Bel", is briefly as follows: Hayk was a son of Togarmah (Til-Garimmu — House of T'orgom), but was living in Babylonia. After the birth of his firstborn Aramanyak (this means, after the establishment of a proto-Armenian kingdom within the country of Aram), Hayk left Babylonia and travelled northwards to the south of Lake Van, where he established a 'house' (city) which he entrusted to his grandson Kadmos (this is a reference to the city of Hubushkia in Kadmukhi where Dadi, known as Kadmos, ruled). After this event Hayk travelled north-west and settled in the Hark' district, to the north of Lake Van. (Remarkably, the direction of Hayk's travel is correct, but his place of settlement was wrongly given, because from Hubushkia Lake Van is directly to the north and at that time there was no Hark' district; whereas Kiaka (Zabgaga) was exactly to the north-west of Hubushkia). He established a village in Hark' district which he named Haykashen (built by Hayk) after himself.

THE PRE-HISTORY OF THE ARMENIANS

The Progeny of Hayk

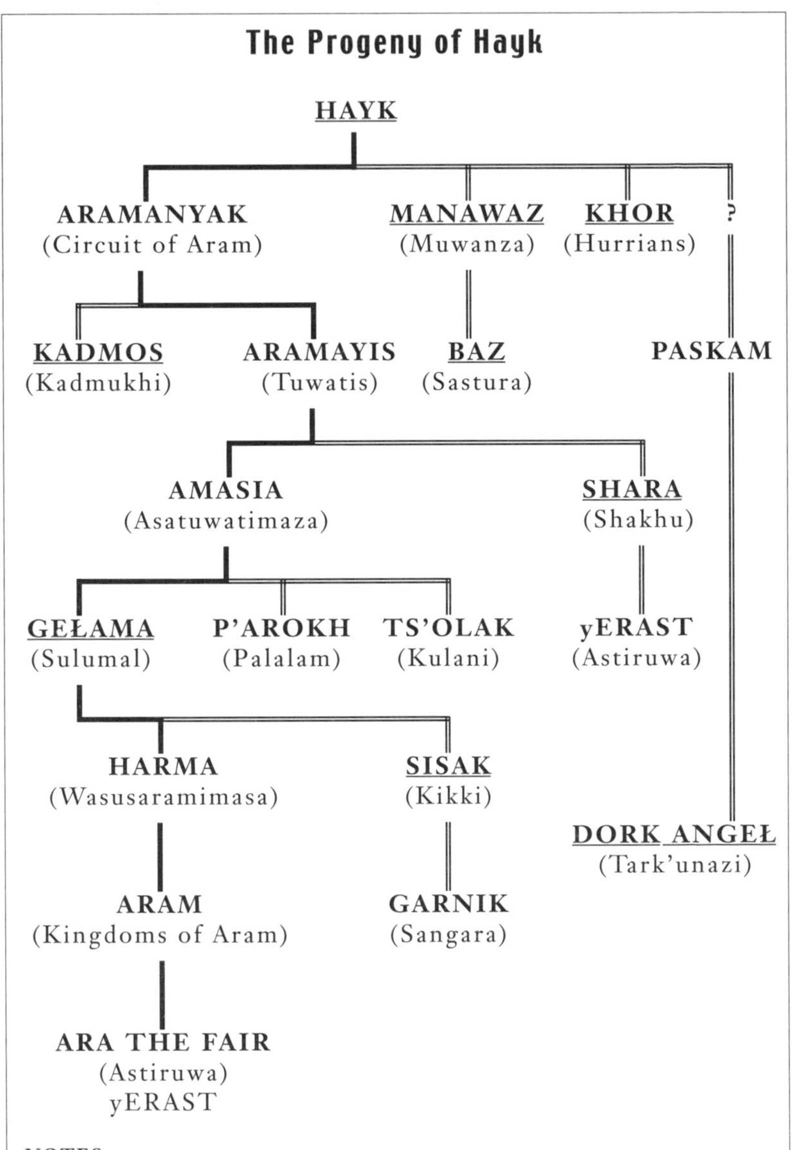

NOTES
1. The solid line represents the longest line of kings according to Khorenats'i. This line also appears in Sebeos' history, chapter 1.
2. The underlined names represent future dukedoms and are the members of the original Ostan organisation.
3. Two dukedoms are attributed to Shara: the Shahunis and the Gusharids.

Bel, the king of Assyria, sent an embassy to Hayk asking him to return, which he refused to do. In response Bel raised an army and launched an expedition to the north in order to punish Hayk. Hayk, too, collected his men regrouping by a salty lake where the battle plans were discussed. After travelling many more miles, Hayk and his men arrived at a plain surrounded by high mountains on the right side of running water (Euphrates[?]). They positioned themselves on a secure high-ground and the battle started, in the course of which Bel was killed by Hayk's own arrow, despatched from his "crooked and wide-opening bow" (this is also the description of the Paeonian bow in the *Iliad* 2.982). The Assyrian army dispersed leaving behind much booty. Hayk buried Bel on a high mountain, a place which became known as the 'cemeteries' (this is a reference to Mount Nemrud where the princes of Kummukh had been buried from times immemorial).[2]

Khorenatsi does not know to what period the battle of Hayk and Bel belongs. It can now be confirmed that it took place in the last decade of the 8th century BC, when there was no Armenia, Hark' district, or Haykashen village, because at that date all these lands were part of the Urartian kingdom.

Cuneiform sources

There is no Assyrian version of the story of the battle of Hayk and Bel, but there are three cuneiform sources, which help us to construct the events of 705 BC, which confirm what Khorenatsi had written. But first we must establish that the king called Bel was actually Sargon II (722-705 BC). In the Assyrian history only two kings died abroad. These two were Sargon II and his grandson Esarhaddon. Esarhaddon died from sickness on his way to Egypt, but Sargon had a soldier's death in Tabal. The Babylonian Chronicle No. 1, relates that "on his 17th year (of reign) Sargon marched to Tabal".[3] A fragment of an Assyrian inscription, in connection with Sargon's death, reads: "(The king) went against Eshpai, the Kulumean, he was killed, and the camp of the king (dispersed)" — the tablet is broken at this point. It is fortunate that there is a third inscription named the Kuyunjik Collection, Letter 129, which throws more light on the subject. This is the letter of Sargon's plenipotentiary, a man known as Mannuki-Ninua. The parts of the letter that concerns this study reads as follows: "Regarding the people of Zabgaga, of whom the King my Lord has written, I shall inquire. I have seen where they go out and in. Send (thither). Now they have departed from the house of Dalta. They have entered into the city of the Kuluman tribe with their kinsmen (and) dwell (there). And when I arrived (and) had established the oath the people of Kuluman, they restored the prefecture. They are with the governor. They are at peace. On account of the city of Zabgaga they have besought me" . . . "whatever news of the people of Zabgaga you hear, send to me."[4]

The translator of this inscription, in his commentary, says: "Kuluman was a loyal Assyrian city, near the south-eastern borders"; and for Zabgaga: "apparently it belonged in Armenian territory". The translator's comments that Kuluman was a city near the south-eastern borders of Assyria can be accepted, as this part of Assyria is the farthest geographical point from Tabal, where the Assyrians could have relocated Eshpai (Hayk), if Sargon in one of his previous campaigns in Tabal had seized and taken the population of Zabgaga to Assyria. However, the claim that Zabgaga was a place in Armenian territory is confusing, because no such city had ever been known in Armenia, and furthermore at that time there was no such a country as Armenia. The fact is that Sargon advanced against Tabal and that is where this place must be found.

We do not know of a place named Zabgaga in Tabal, and no other source mentions this place name, except Letter 129 under discussion. But, fortunately, the word 'Zabgaga' can be explained in the Armenian language, which may enable us to find the city under a different name, because, as we have seen in the case of other names, in recompositions the sense of the original word is always kept. The word 'Zabgaga' is a compound of 'zab' + 'ga' + 'ga' and means 'a palm size place where there is life', in other words a small habitation full of life ('zab' > 'tsap'' = 'palm (of the hand' — the proto-Armenian 'z' = 'ts'', a dative case prefix) + 'ga' > 'ka' = there is, exists — the same stem is repeated; therefore 'a palm-sized place where there is habitation'.

Zabgaga is the same place as the city of Kiaka of the time of the Artaxiad kingdom, known at the present as the Karahöyük ruins, near the town of Arguvan, approximately 60 km north of Melid as the crow flies. The first word of the ancient compound, Zab, has been discarded, as it states the obvious: anybody could see that it was a small place. The meaning of Kiaka is the same as Zabgaga minus the word 'palm' ('kia' = 'life' + 'ka' = 'there is' — the 'ka' is the same stem found in Zabgaga). The correlation of 'there is life' with the '(palm-sized place where) there is life' is perfect. Zabgaga appears to have been within the juristiction of either Togarmah or Melid, which means the battle of Sargon and Eshpai took place elsewhere, because the Babylonian Chronicle says that Sargon marched on Tabal, though Khorenatsi is of the opinion that the battle took place to the west of a river which would place the battlefield somewhere in Kummukh.

It is obvious that Khorenatsi had woven his tale around place names of Hark', where the 'fathers' lived, and the village name of Haykashen, built by Hayk. Lacking the necessary information he did not realise that these place names belonged to a different era and to a different people, as we shall see.

The short Assyrian inscription relating to the death of Sargon calls Hayk 'Eshpai the Kulumean', of which the Armenian tradition was not aware. According to the letter of Mannuki-Ninua (Letter 129), Eshpai and his people had entered the city of Kuluman and lived there until they managed to escape to their own lands, which, because of the time they had lived in the city of Kuluman, earned Eshpai the epithet 'the Kulumean'.

CHAPTER 13

HAYK'S PROGENY

Lists of kings and rulers

Khorenatsi in Book I records the names of the great figures in proto-Armenian history in three lists. Of these, the third list (1.22) is the most orderly and, in the main, comprises the names of the Cilician rulers. The first list (1.12) represents the rulers whom he calls "Hayk's progeny". His second list (I.19) comprises the names of the various rulers of Aram, whom he refers as "the branches of our nation after Aram". The names contained in the second list appear at first sight to be arbitrarily left out of the first list, because both the first and second list contain the names of the rulers of Aram. In this chapter we will deal with the first name-list, which is known as "the ancient Haykid kings".

The label of "Haykid kings" is misleading, because the names contained in all the three name-lists are those of Haykid kings; Haykid means true proto-Armenian. However, the division between the first and the second lists is intentional, even though such an arrangement does not represent a true historical situation, because, there are cases where a son appears in the first list and the father appears in the second. Also, there were rulers who because of their antiquity one would expect to find in the first list and are instead relegated to the second. But the most objectionable shortcoming of these lists must be their arrangement, which adheres neither to a chronological order nor to a true dynastic line, which makes the information rather confusing.

Irrespective of these shortcomings, the first name-list is a remarkable collection, a masterpiece of perpetuating oral history. The unknown genius who had compiled and recomposed these names, taking them from Mar Aba's book, knew exactly how to arrange them in order to inform the future generations of their prehistory. It is clear that Khorenatsi had no part in the compilation of any of the lists, because, he does not show any understanding of the purpose behind their organisation, nor does he know any of the archaic names. His main achievement has been to combine the legends, which were circulating in the highlands of Armenia during the Classical Armenian period, with what Mar Aba's edited book had recorded about the earlier proto-Armenian rulers. Still, it is a matter for wonderment how he had managed to get hold of such a wealth of information.

It is not known exactly when the names of these lists were recomposed and compiled in their present forms; but it is certain that they belong to the Classical Armenian period between the second century BC and the fourth century AD.

Names from the Armenian traditions

The Assyrians, Babylonians, Urartians and the hieroglyphic inscriptions of the tenth to sixth centuries BC give us the most archaic forms of these names. The main source is that of the Assyrian inscriptions. However, none of these sources mention the names of Khor, Aramanyak, Kadmos and Aram. This is because the first name is the Armenian rendering of the ethnonym Hurrian, and the remaining three names are all toponyms. It is only the Armenian traditions that present these names to us as belonging to historical personages. The reason for this anomaly was the fact that in oral history it is always easier to arrange names in a pyramidal style, similar to the example of Noah's sons in the Bible.

The most striking aspect of the first list is that the compiler knew when all the old kingdoms represented by the names had come to an end, which we now know was in the last quarter of the 8th century BC, the time when Assyrians, under Sargon II, suppressed south-eastern Anatolia and imposed their own governors or client rulers. That is the first reason for the presentation of the first name-list as Hayk's progeny; even though the division between the names of Hayk's progeny and the names after Aram (the second name-list) is not perfect, because as already mentioned, there are other ancient proto-Armenian kingdoms, such as the kingdom of Kummukh, which came to an end at the same time as the Haykid kingdoms, and yet none of these rulers are included in the first list. The second reason for the exclusion of kings, even entire dynasties, from the first list of Haykid names is indeed the most valuable element of the compilation, since the comparison of the lists and a few valid inferences based on known facts give us the history of the proto-Armenian entry into Urartu, an account of the most ancient Ostan confederation, the name of the 'Fathers' after whom a district was named Hark', and the name of the supreme commander of the proto-Armenian forces. There is no other source that sheds light on the history of the proto-Armenian entry into Urartu.

It is clear that by Khorenatsi's time the population of Armenia had forgotten whom and what the recomposed names of the lists had represented (it is a fact that even some of the recomposed names are beyond the understanding of present day scholarship), except that these were the ancient kings of the Armenians. This is misleading, because Armenians can only belong to a time when there was a country of Armenia. Khorenatsi, too, makes the same mistake, due to not having outside sources available to him (Mar Aba's book recorded only the names and some details taken from the Assyrian sources). Therefore, being unable to penetrate the meaning and the purpose of the lists he forms the opinion that all the later dukedoms carrying the dynastic names of the ancient kings must have been established by them personally, and consequently, that everything that had taken place in the past had its origins on the soil of Armenia. It appears that he had overlooked what he himself had written about Tigran Sakawakeats "extending the borders of Armenia as far as the extreme edges of the countries of ancient proto-Armenian habitation" (1.24) and had ignored the fact that Togarmah (House of T'orgom), too, was outside of Armenia.

Early Armenian Arsacid history records dukedoms and ducal dynasties bearing the same names as those of Hayk's progeny over 500 years after the proto-Armenian entry into Urartu. Before the Arsacids most of the descendants of these royal houses must have been known as Ark'unik' (Royal Family), which means that by organizing these royal 'houses' into dukedoms, the Arsacids were actually diminishing their status. And, at the same time they were elevating some of the Urartian, Mardian, Median, Assyrian and ancient Persian families to the same status of dukedom. This has added to the confusion involving the pedigree of the various Armenian 'Houses', and the fact that, it was about this time that the Arsacids usurped to themselves the most prestigious designation of Ostan, has added to the confusion.[5]

THE NAMES OF HAYK'S PROGENY

Aramanyak

He was the eldest son of Hayk, and himself had two sons, of which the first was Kadmos and the second Aramayis. It was stated above that Aramanyak and Kadmos were not personal names, but toponyms. In later Armenia we do not find a dukedom under the name of Aramanyak, nor do we find any such place name, except that, as Khorenatsi claims, Aramanyak had named the mount Aragats after himself. This makes no sense linguistically and is not acceptable. The name is connected with Aragats in order to show that Aramanyak is remembered in Armenia, which conforms to the underlying plan, as we will see below. Aramanyak is a compound word consisting from 'Aram' + 'manyak', which means the 'circuit of Aram' ('Aram' = the name of the country of south-eastern Anatolia + 'manyak' = 'a necklace, bracelet, circle, etc').

In Book 1.20 Khorenatsi makes one of his most interesting statements concerning Anushawan (...ussi, discussed in Chapter 6, page 100). He writes that "Anushawan was dedicated to the cult of the plane trees of Aramanyak in Armawir city". He does not understand his own revelation and cannot be blamed for it, because at the time he was writing his history, the memory of the country of Aram and the proto-Armenian habitation there, were long forgotten. In the sentence quoted above, the plane trees of Aramanyak are those in the area around Aram, in south-eastern Anatolia. There has never been an Aramanyak, or a forest of Aramanyak, in the city of Armawir in Armenia.

Khor

He was the second son of Hayk, which confers seniority upon him, even though he was not of true proto-Armenian descent, which can be inferred from the fact that Khor is not allocated a progeny. It is certain that Khor represents the Hurrian population of Carchemish, who by the time the proto-Armenians moved into Urartu, were completely armenicised and were one of the members of the Ostan confederation, as we will see.

The fact that Khor is made a son of Hayk reflects the importance of the armenicised Hurrians,[6] who, after entry into Urartu were one of the tripartite core of the central council of the Ostan confederation. Their place of settlement in Armenia comprised the entire northern coastal lands of Lake Van, bordering the Urartians to the east, the Bznunians to the west and the Manawazians to the north.

This house of Khor became known as the dukedom of the Khorkhorunik'. The Khorkhorunik' during the Arsacid rule, were made Malkhaz and by tradition the Commanders of the King's bodyguard. The 'House' of Khorkhorunik' lasted as a dukedom until the middle of the seventh century AD, that is until the time of the Arab invasions of Armenia.

Manawaz

This is the Muwazisa of Gurgum (Marash) as we saw previously (Chapter 5, page 84). He was the third son of Hayk, and the oldest proto-Armenian ruler Khorenatsi records. The dynasty of Gurgum took on the name of Muwazisa (it was Muwazisa's father, Larazamasa, who had established the rulership) and in Armenia became known as the Royal House of Manawazians, centred on the fortress city of Mana(wa)zkert with their large state bordering both Khorkhorunik' and the Bznunians to the south. The Royal House of Manawazians were the leaders of the proto-Armenian forces entering Urartu, which was the reason for their state being called Hark' (= 'where fathers live' — 'father' = 'leader, most senior, etc'). The supreme commander was Haykak Manawazian, after whom the village of Haykashen was named.

The Manawazians, at the time of the Arsacid kings of Armenia, were relegated to the status of a dukedom, and were never entrusted with a high position in the administration. In fact, due to the high popular esteem they commanded, the Arsacids considered them a threat to their rule and when the opportunity arose it was politically expedient for the Arsacid Chosrov Kodak (AD 330-38) to have them annihilated. The Manawazian lands were granted to bishop Ałbianos, which sealed the demise of the Manawazians. The gentilitial Manawazian House lasted from the 10th century BC to the 4th century AD.

Baz or Bazuk

As seen previously (Chapter 4, page 80), his proto-Armenian name was Sastura, the prime minister of Kamana of Carchemish. The successor of Kamana, his youngest brother Pisiris, was exiled to Assyria together with his family, by Sargon II in 717 BC. The descendants of Baz appear to have escaped deportation and became the leading princely 'house' of Carchemish.

At the time of the proto-Armenians' move into Urartu the Carchemisheans, as members of the Ostan confederation, had participated under the banner of the Baz. They settled to the north-west of Lake Van, as one of the tripartite council, but in a role secondary to that of the Manawazians, which is the reason why Khorenatsi makes Baz the son of Manawaz. Their area of settlement, in what was later to become Armenia, was named the country of Bznunians, and Lake Van was renamed after them as the Bznunian sea.

At the time of the Arsacid reorganization of Armenia the House of the Bznunians was made into a dukedom under the same name, which lasted into the second quarter of the 4th century AD, enduring some 1,100 years. The 'house' of Bznunians was another dukedom which had its demise under the Arsacid Chosrov Kodak. The last known patriarch of this clan was Dat'abē, who was executed (Faustos 3.8).

Kadmos

He represents the patriarchal house of the Kadmeans, the most obscure of all the dukedoms. No other ancient writer records this name, except Sebēos of 7th century AD, who had taken his material from Khorenatsi.

Khorenatsi in Book 1.10-12 shows Kadmos as a son of Aramanyak, which means that the rulership of Kadmukhi (actually the name of the city was Hubushkia) was a singular offshoot of the proto-Armenians in the country of Aram. Therefore, Kadmos can be speculatively connected with Dadi of Hubushkia, as we have no knowledge of any other claimants. Dadi was the only proto-Armenian to rule in Hubushkia at the time of Shamshi-Adad V (823-810 BC) of Assyria. After Dadi the rulership of the country reverted to the Hurrians, which may be inferred from the names of the rulers recorded by the Assyrians. This must be the reason for Khorenatsi to ascribe no progeny to Kadmos.

In Book 1.14 Khorenatsi says that the descendants of Kadmos, the Kadmeans, were the keepers of the southern borders (the Assyrian march) of Armenia. What Khorenatsi writes is the total sum of what we know. There are no other sources to confirm whether the nobility of the ex-royal house of Dadi lasted into the early Arsacid era. However, we know from Xenophon that at his crossing of the River Centrites, his army was opposed by Armenians and others. It is possible that these Armenians were under the overlordship of the descendants of Dadi. The presence of the Armenians in these parts of the country, under the leadership of a nobility is an essential historical requirement in order to complete the pattern of circumvention of the entire highlands. In Book 2.8 Khorenatsi says that "the Kadmeans (south) together with the Sisakeans (east) were entrusted the protection of the borders to the extreme edges of the country, where the Armenian language ceases to be spoken."

The Armenian population of Kadmukhi under the Kadmeans would not have been very numerous until the arrival of the Gordynian and Mygdonian proto-Armenians from the Balkans in the course of the 4th to 2nd centuries BC. These newcomers settled in and around Nisibis (Mtsbin); their places of settlement became known as Gordyene and Mygdonia, perpetuating the name of the Paeonian districts they had left behind in the Balkans. At about this time the dukedom of the Kadmeans became a mighty power, which is reflected in the "respective military potential of the princes of Armenia", wherein the princes of the Vitaxae of Adiabene, who were the inheritors of the Kadmean lands, were credited with a cavalry of some 13,200 warriors.

By the end of the second century BC the Kadmean jurisdiction over their lands had ceased; because, the Parthians had overrun the country and the first branch of the Arsacids was established in Nisibis covering the districts of Adiabene, Gordyene and Mygdonia, which were under the hegemony of Atropatene.[7] Around AD 66 a new Arsacid dynasty started in Armenia proper, but the Kadmeans had disappeared a century or so before that.

Aramayis
He was the second son of Aramanyak, but in history he was the great King Tuwatis of Tabal. Hayk's grandchildren, Kadmos and Baz, had no progeny, and the patriarchal line was carried on by the third grandson, Aramayis. This distinction, in the composition of the Haykid list, was due to the fact that Tuwatis

was the most senior king of his time and used the title of great king (this title, in proto-Armenian, can be seen in inscription Tabal I.6c written as 'apawa' > 'awaga' = 'senior').

According to Khorenatsi, in later Armenia, the name of Aramayis was connected with the city of Armawir. While there may be a phonetic similarity, linguistically the connection makes no sense.

Shara

He was the first born of Aramayis, in the Haykid list. In reality he was Shakhu/Shadawale of Melid of the 9th century BC. Khorenatsi ascribes to him just one son, Erast (Astiruwa), with whom the dynastic line ends.

To Shara (Shakhu) Khorenatsi does not ascribe a dukedom, as he had done for the other 'Houses'. In fact, he does not mention Shaheans at all, but always refers to "Shara's descendants" (2.4), "Shara's borders" (2.6) and "Shara's sons" (2.8). Perhaps, after the Shara/Shirak correlation he had deemed it unnecessary to add another familial epithet, but Khorenatsi must have known the name of the dukedom as the Shaheans, which appear in Faustos's history as Shahēi (3.9), Shahuni (3.12) and Shahunots (4.24). However, the name Shahean or Shahuni appears to be a euphemism, because the 'kh' of Shakhu has been changed to 'h', which instead of usury, conveys the sense of legitimate profit.

Khorenatsi connects the Shaheans to the Sisakeans and the Kadmeans in order to confirm a patriarchal or true proto-Armenian derivation, which he also ascribes to the Gusharids of northern Armenia (of Shirak district and north). In 22.4, Gushar is shown to be a son of a son of Shara, therefore, two dukedoms derive from Shara, the Shaheans and the Gusharids.

The descendants of Shara were one of the original members of the Ostan confederation, which can also be ascribed to the Gusharids by proxy, since they appear to have originated in later Armenia.

We lose sight of the Shaheans in the last quarter of the 4th century AD, when western Armenia was annexed to Byzantium. It is possible that the 'House of Shara' survived up to the beginning of the 7th century under Byzantine rule. All the same, the name of Shakhu, recomposed as Shara, has lasted at least 1,500 years.

Amasia

Amasia was the second son of Aramayis in the Haykid list. In reality he was a much older king than Aramayis or the elder brother Shara. We know him as Asatuwatimaza of Carchemish of the 10th century BC.

Khorenatsi mentions that the mountain of Masis (Ararat) was named after this Amasia, which does not make sense. If anything, Masis may mean 'part of Sis' or 'belonging to the Sisakans', because originally the territory of this 'House' was far larger and the mountain of Masis was part of it.

According to the name-list, Amasia had three sons, Gełama, P'arokh and Ts'olak. To the last two sons he made gifts of land by Mount Ararat (Masis), but it was Gełama who continued the dynastic line.

Erast

Erast, Astiruwa of Carchemishean history, was the only son of Shara, therefore, a grandson of Aramayis in the Haykid list. Khorenatsi tells us that Aramayis renamed the river Arak'si after his grandson, Erast, as Eraskh, which makes no sense linguistically.

Erast and Ara the Fair are the same person, so this name will therefore be further discussed under the name of Ara the Fair.

Ts'olak

This is the recomposed name of Kulani, a eunuch governor of Unqi (Patinu) at the time of Tiglath-Pileser III of Assyria. In

Khorenatsi's history he is the third son of Amasia and inherited the village of Ts'olakert.

P'arokh

This is the recomposed name of Palalam of the Assyrian inscriptions[8] and Larazamasa of the hieroglyphics (Inscription Marash I). There have been two rulers with this name, the first was the founder of the Gurgum dynasty and the second his great-great-great-grandson. The first Palalam is not known to the Assyrians, therefore, this P'arokh is the second ruler known under this name. In Khorenatsi's history he is the second son of Amasia. P'arokh and his descendants were known as Manawazians (belonging to the dynasty of Muwazisa) which must be the reason for his not being ascribed to any position in Armenia nor assigned any progeny. It is said only that he inherited the village of P'arakhod from his father Amasia.

Gełam

He was the first son of Amasia. As a historical figue he is the Sulumal of Melid (the son of Khelaruada who is absent from the Haykid list) of the Assyrian inscription. Gełam's descendants claimed the lands to the west and north of Lake Lychnidus (present Sevan) in Armenia, which was much later renamed after Gełam as Lake Gełama and the lands they settled in became known as the district of Gełark'unik'.

Before the proto-Armenians' move into Urartu, when the descendants of the various ex-royal houses were concluding their agreement as to which district each would settle, the Gełark'unik' must have opted for the north-east of the highlands, where a large number of their people had been formerly relocated by Menua, Sarduri and Argishti of Urartu. This made the north-east of the highlands one of the most densely populated areas, which can also be inferred from the fact that most of the capital cities of Armenia were situated in those parts, though there were other reasons, too, for this choice.

Gełark'unik' is the only member of the Ostan confederation that always kept the 'ark'unik'' ('royal family') epithet and never became a dukedom, because, before the era of the Arsacid rulers, this 'House' had already ceased to be, though their name continues to be used, up to the present, for Lake Sevan, which is also referred to as Lake Gełama, and the mountains to the west of the lake which are known as the Geł Mountains.

The reason for the demise of this great House must be the fact that when, early in the second century BC the Artaxiad dynasty was established in the city of Armawir in Armenia, the rulers and this House were sharing the same territory. This means that the Gełark'unik' were deprived of their lands and were absorbed and disappeared from the scene — for without lands what significance would a noble house have? These must be the reason why Agathangełos, Faustos and P'arpetsi do not mention the name of Gełark'unik'.

It has been suggested that Gełark'unik' of Khorenatsi and Ŭelikuni of the Urartian inscriptions are the same. This speculation has no foundation in history nor in language. There have also been efforts to derive the name from the word 'giwł' and 'gewł' meaning a village. A 'village lake' and a 'village mountain' sound rather nonsensical.

Sisak

This is the Kikki of Shalmaneser's inscription, but in Khorenatsi's history he is the son of Gełam, who gave him the larger share of his lands, meaning that the Sisakeans had the larger part of the eastern Armenian highlands. With the establishment of the Artaxiads in Armawir, and later the move of the capital city to the newly built Artaxiada, the Sisakeans lost much of their territory to the south and south-west of Lake Lychnidus (Sevan). Still later, under the Arsacids, the whole of their district was reorganized as the principality of Siwnik', wherein Sisakan remained just the name of a canton, even though the ex-royal family of Sisak was still the head of the new country, which we know from Koriwn (*Life of Mashtots*, 14), who is the first to commemorate the name of Sisakan.[9]

The population of Sisakan were the old Tabalian proto-Armenians, who had originally come from Pelagonia and settled in the various districts of Tabal. They were members of the Ostan confederation and after their move into the eastern highlands of Urartu, they had named the present-day Lake Sevan Lychnidus, after the one they had left behind in Pelagonia. The principality of the Sisakeans lasted longer than any other proto-Armenian derived 'House', though under the name of Siwnik' and under the leadership of other families.

Garnik

He was, according to Khorenatsi, the son of Sisak (Kikki) and the last of the line. He was of course the Sangara of Carchemish of the Assyrian inscriptions, and had no relaltionship with Kikki of Tabal.

Khorenatsi says that Gełam, Garnik's grandfather, had built a city and named it Gełami. This city was presented to Garnik, who renamed it Garni after himself. Garni and Garnik have similar phonetics but it is not possible to correlate them. Garni is the Armenian rendering of the Urartian place name known as Giarniani. In the Haykid list Garnik was not ascribed a progeny, but Khorenatsi adds that the later Varažnunis were his descendants. This extrapolation belongs to later times and it is not related nor does it affect the Haykid name-list.

Harma

As seen in the previous chapter, this is the name of the great king of Tabal, Wasusaramimasa. The name having been taken from the Assyrian inscriptions, where it appears as Uasusarma, the compiler of the list has transcribed only the 'sarma' part as Harma, who, according to Khorenatsi, was Gełam's first son. Harma, himself, was the 'father' of Aram, which means he was the most senior king among the proto-Armenian rulers of the country of Aram. This last piece of information has been misunderstood and some have resorted to the simplistic choice of making Aram a person and Harma his real father!

Sometime between 732 and 729 BC Harma was dethroned by Tiglath-Pileser III of Assyria, which must be the reason for the absence of any progeny of his in Armenia.

Aram

He was Harma's son, whom Khorenatsi calls Aram, attributing to him many brave deeds, because of which historians have regarded him as Aramé, first king of Urartu! The assumption has no historical basis and, as previously pointed out, Aram was only the name of the country wherein the proto-Armenians had various rulers. Khorenatsi tells us that it was after the name of this Aram that "other nations called us Armenians" (Book I.12 and 14), which agrees with the statement of Flavius Josephus that the Armenians were the sons of Aram.[10] As for the long list of rulers that follows, Khorenatsi classes them as the "branches of our nation", which, again, means the various rulers of the country of Aram. Aram and the Aram of the Aramanyak cannot be explained in the Armenian language, as it is the archaic name of the country, coming down from the times of Naram-Sin of Akkad (23rd century BC),[11] which the Armenians continued to use well into the 5th century AD.[12] The word *Armenian* did not even exist in the Armenian vocabulary until recent times.

The brave deeds attributed to Aram have taken place between the period of 780 to 590 BC, which itself makes it obvious that the country's name is used because the oral history from which Khorenatsi had gleaned his information had long forgotten to which ruler a particular deed belonged. Khorenatsi admits his dependence on oral sources, and adds that "these acts and events were not recorded by the inscriptions of kings (referring to the Assyrian sources) nor by the hieroglyphics" (Book 1.14).

Armenian means the people of Aram. The second unaccented 'a' of Aram has been dropped, as was also the case with Teg-aramah and Tog-armah.

Ara the Fair

He is the last of the line of the Haykid list, presented as the son of Aram. Ara the Fair and Erast ('Astir-uwa') are the same person, who was discussed in the previous chapter (page 77) for Carchemish.

The colourful story of Ara the Fair is a romance based on some valid facts, which are:

a) he died young;
b) that he left behind a twelve-year-old son;
c) that Arayan Ara (Yarairaisa) became the caretaker of the state; and d) his widow's name was Nuard, which correlates with the name we know from A 7 inscription of Yarairaisa, with Tuwarasaisa.

Oral history is the source of this story, which means there is much fiction interwoven with the above facts and additionally, the story is ignorant of the fact that Ara the Fair and Erast were the same person. Khorenatsi, having taken his material from the oral sources, is also unaware that the two names belong to the same person, which is why this ruler appears twice in the Haykid list. Also, the oral source, and consequently Khorenatsi, identifies Arayan Ara with the twelve year old son as caretaker of the state, being unaware of Kamana (Hawanak), who appears in the second list.

The story of Ara the Fair is a mythical romance and makes use of what Ctesias, who is reproduced in Diodorus Siculus, tells us about Semiramis, the widow of Shamshi-Adad V, that she desired him because of his handsomeness but was rejected. To get her own way Semiramis attacked Ara, but gave instructions to seize him alive. However, Ara fell in the battle and died. The oral story makes a moral point, but never deifies Ara or any other person. Remarkably, the deification of Ara is due to modern scholars, who have transformed him into a figure of fire and regeneration, compared him with Aris and even with Er (son of the Thessalian Armenius of Plato's Republic, X.614), who unexpectedly becomes an Armenian! Furthermore a constellation is supposed to have been named after him, but which one? The Latin name Ara, for the Greek 'Thytērion' (Armenian 'Zohasełan') — the altar on which gods swore allegiance to Zeus before his fight with Kronos[13] — had nothing to do with the story of Ara the Fair.

The chronology of the period Ara the Fair or Erast belong to, can be reconstructed with the help of the Armenian tradition and the hieroglyphic inscriptions A 6, A 7 and A 15b of Yarairaisa and the Körkün inscription of Ilapikasa. If we accept that the son of Astiruwa was 12 years old (this can be supported by the Yarairaisa relief) when Astiruwa died, and allow for Kamana a reign of 30 years until the succession of the youngest son Pisiris in 738 BC, we end up with a date of 768, and 42 years for the life of Kamana. It follows that c. 770 BC is a good estimate for the death of Astiruwa (Erast or Ara the Fair), which will coincide with the reign of Ashur-dan III.

Tork' Angeł
The Haykid list of Khorenatsi's Book 1.12 does not mention this ruler. In order to remedy the omission, the name appears later, in Book 1.23, as that of a descendant from another branch of Hayk's progeny. It was imperative that this name should be connected with Hayk; otherwise, the list would not have revealed the intricate design of the oral history, which, in this case, is directly preoccupied with the Ostan confederation.

In Book 2.8, Khorenatsi describes Tork' Angeł as a powerful giant of a man, but unshapely and ugly (this is due to the misunderstanding of the word unGeł, which in ancient Classical Armenian had the sense of not noble).[14] Tork' Angeł was a historical figure in the person of Tarkunazi, the ruler of Melid, which in 712 BC became an Assyrian province.

The descendants of this ruler claimed the lands at the source of the Tigris (Ingilene) east of Melid, and became known, in Armenia, as the House of Angels (Angeł Tun), where perhaps they worshipped the south-eastern Anatolian chief god Tark.

Because of Tork' Angeł's theophoric name, many scholars have ascribed to him a divinity. Furthermore, the name of the domain of Angeł Tun many have changed to Angł. It seems that only Khorenatsi, our original and only source, who is level-headed enough to deny the divinity and the superhuman feats of Tork' Angeł, unlike Bishop Sebēos of 7th century AD, whose prehisitory (Chapters 1 and 2) is the unreflecting and mixed-up recollections of his schooldays,[15] which nevertheless earned him the accolade of certain scholars.

The stronghold of the descendants of Tork' Angeł was called Angeł Berd (Angeł Castle) in the south-west of Armenia. During the Artaxiad and Arsacid eras this principality was practically a minor kingdom, governing their enclave and supplying the kings of Armenia with contingents of cavalry. Khorenatsi ascribes them membership to the Ostan confederation because of the sister of king Tigran, who had taken up residence in the castle of Angeł. Khorenatsi is unaware that the Ostan membership of this 'House' was far more ancient than his sources had indicated.

The principality of Angeł Tun lasted almost to the end of the 4th century AD, until the partition of Armenia between Byzantium and the Sassanians. Angeł Tun was in the Byzantine part of this partition and lasted until the 6th century AD, which means that the dynastic name of Angeł, starting with Tarkunazi in the 8th century BC, had lasted over 1200 years, first as the House of Tarkunazi, and after the recomposition of the name, as Angeł Tun.[16]

CHAPTER 15

THE OSTAN CONFEDERATION

Ostan and Ostanik

In ancient Armenian historical manuscripts the words Ostan and Ostanik appear in the works of various authors of the 5th century AD and onwards. The history of Agathangełos, the oldest document to come down to us, does not mention these words. The history of Faustos P'uzandatsi, the second oldest work to have reached us, mentions Ostan only once. Ełishē mentions Ostanik twice and Łazar P'arpetsi eighteen times.

For Armenian history it is important to find out in what context and in what sense the words Ostan and Ostanik were used by the above three authors, and compare the findings with the explanations of various recent scholars. Finally, we must compare all the answers with what Movses Khorenatsi had written during the second half of the 5th century AD.

This method of inquiry is prompted by the fact that, although all the authors mentioned belong to the 5th century AD or thereabouts, Khorenatsi is the only one who had written the history of the Armenians from the beginning up to nearly his own time; whereas, the others had written histories only of their own times. Of course, there were other later writers, too, who referred to Ostan and Ostanik, but their views are based on what these ancient historians had written, are therefore mere repetitions, and of no particular interest to us.

Faustos (4.19) tells us that "the king, Arshak II (AD 350-68), put the clan of Kamsarakan to death, who were the masters of Shirak and Arsharunik districts, and assigned the lands to the Ostan", which means the lands of Kamsarakan became crown property.

Ełishē (ch.1) tells us that "the Persian king, Yazdajird II (AD 438-57), was enlisting soldiers for his army from the nobility and freemen, and from the king's properties, known as Ostaniks" (at the time there was not an Armenian king, but people still referred to the Ayrarat district as king's property). In Chapter 4, where the names of Vasak's collaborators are given, Ełishē adds that: "Vasak enlisted many collaborators from the freemen and crown properties, known as men of Ostaniks."

Ostanik is the diminutive of Ostan, meaning little ostans, and in those days referred to the various minor Arsacid clans related to the king, who owned estates within the Ayrarat district, which was itself known as crown, or king's, property.

P'arpetsi refers to the new city of Vałarshapat three times as Ostan, the seat of Arsacid kings. There are nine references to the city of Duin, which had replaced Vałarshapat as the Ostan in the time of Chosrov Kodak (AD 330-38). Also, there are five references to the gentry of the Ayrarat district, related to the Arsacids, as Ostaniks. Beside these, there is one anomalous reference to the Ostan Shahastan (2.53), which appears to be a writer's licence that P'arpetsi had allowed himself. Because, Shahastan is the city of Nishapur in the Apar district (the present Neyshābūr to the south-east of the Caspian Sea), which was founded by Shabuh I (AD 241-72); there is nothing in this use of the description Ostan that relates to the Armenians.

In the light of the foregoing analysis, we can now conclude that for these ancient writers Ostan meant a royal city where the court resided and Ostanik represented the gentry of Ayrarat district, who were offshoots of the Arsacids.

However, after the fall of the Arsacid dynasty (AD 428) of

The original Ostan and politico-strategic settlement areas

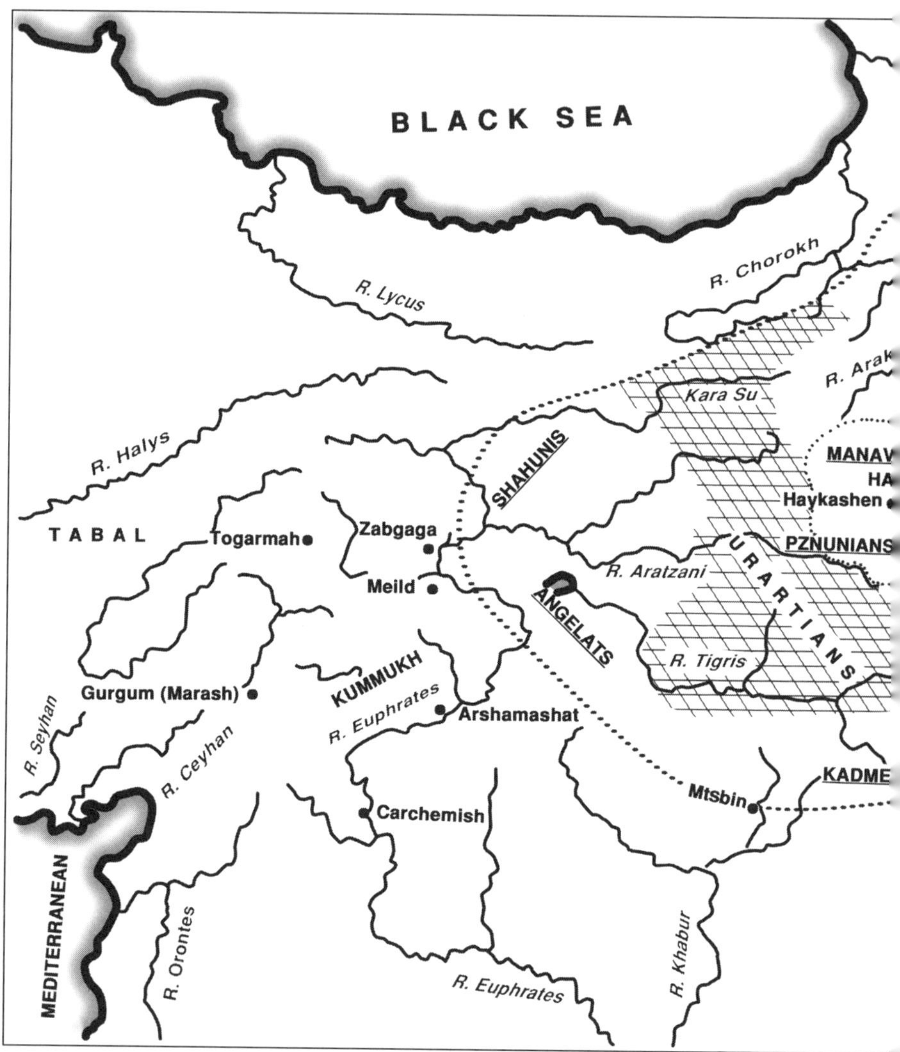

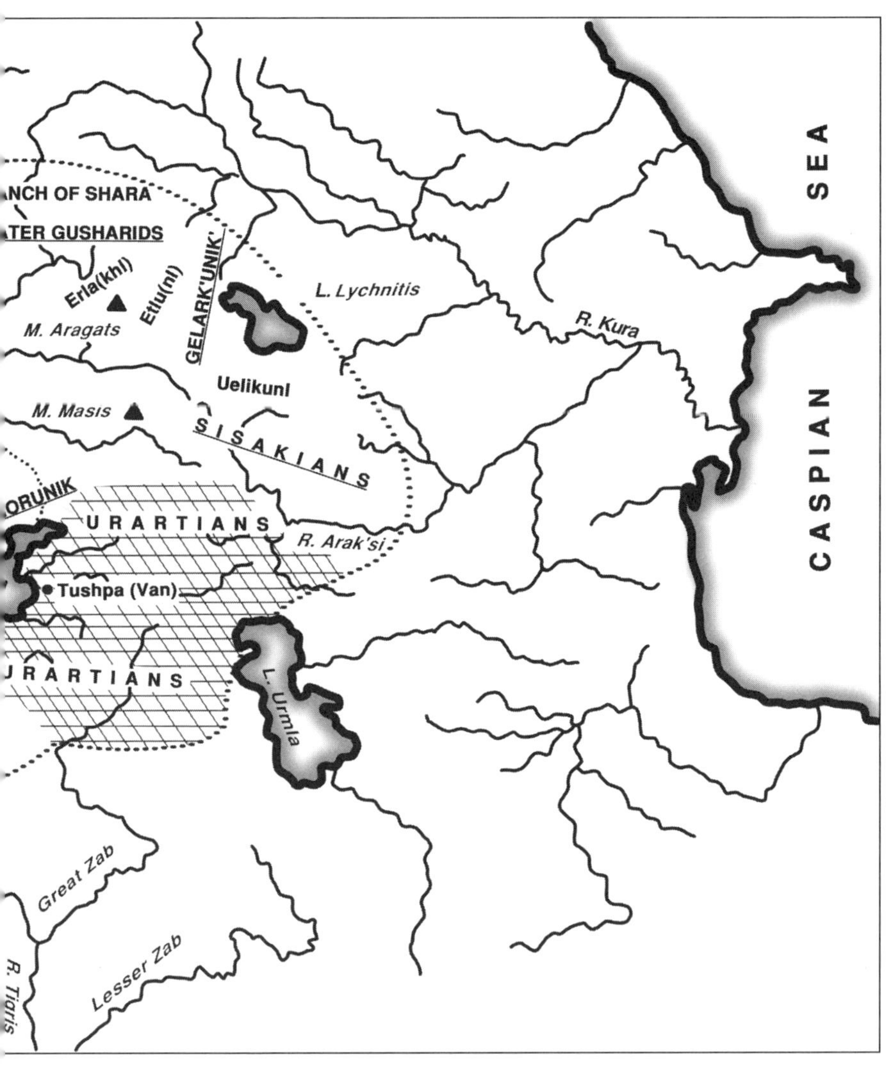

SEA
CASPIAN
NCH OF SHARA
TER GUSHARIDS
Erla(khl)
Etiu(nl)
M. Aragats
GELARK'UNIK'
L. Lychnitis
R. Kura
Uelikunl
M. Masis
S I S A K I A N S
ORUNIK
U R A R T I A N S
R. Arak'si
Tushpa (Van)
U R A R T I A N S
L. Urmla
Great Zab
Lesser Zab
R. Tigris

Armenia, the last capital city of Duin was still called Ostan and the nobility of the Ayrarat district Ostaniks. In other words, Ostan had ceased to be the location of the royal court, but the population and the chroniclers continued to call the principal city Ostan. Further erosion of the meaning of Ostan is seen from the fact that important principalities, such as Daroynk' (Bagratids), Hadamakert (Ardzrunis), Nakhchavan (Vaspurakan) and Ostan city of the Rshtunik' started to use this prestigious designation for themselves. As for Ostanik, this term, too, became looser and many minor dukedoms, unrelated to the Arsacids, assumed the title. It is remarkable that even the language used by the nobility in various centres or courts became known as 'Ostanik language', meaning refined and polite Armenian.

Derivation of Ostan

Of recent scholars Hübschman says that Ostan derives from the Pahlavi 'χostan' and Persian 'ōstandār' with the meaning of 'district overlord'. Malkhazyants' opinion is that Ostan means 'district'; Adontz and Toumanoff say that Ostanik signifies 'men of Ostan' ('courtiers'), and Ostan itself means 'court, residence and threshold'.

Manandyan says that Ostan derives from the Pahlavi 'ōstān', meaning 'district and overlordship', or, from the Persian 'ūstān' or 'āsitan', meaning 'court, residence and threshold'. He adds that: "The title was used during Arsacid reign for royal properties up to AD 428. The Ayrarat district was called Ostan as were also other places belonging to the crown. Nobility and freeman living in Ostans were called Ostaniks, and, after the fall of the Arsacid kingdom the ex-royal city and other large principalities were also called Ostan."

Adjaryan is of the opinion that Ostan is a borrowed word from the Pahlavi and derives from 'ōstāndār', though he admits that the Pahlavi language does not have the stem 'ōstān'. He ascribes to the word the meaning of 'famous royal city'.

All these explanations and meanings make sense, as we have

seen from the quotations taken from the works of the ancient writers. Nevertheless, there are aspects of the matter which I find rather doubtful. Manandyan's generalisation of "during the Arsacid reign" should be changed to *during the mid-Arsacid reign and onwards*, because there is no evidence that the early Arsacids used such a term — as indicated above; the title begins with the new city of Vałarshapat. We must also establish whether or not this title was borrowed from the Pahlavi. Adjaryan's remark that Pahlavi did not have this stem carries more weight than any other opinion, as he was the best linguist that Armenia has produced. Furthermore one might ask if the Ostan title existed before the reign of Chosrov Kodak. We must decide too whether the word Ostan is explainable in the Armenian language, and if so, from which period, and whether it is possible that the Pahlavi had borrowed the word from the Armenians? Answers to these questions will be given below, but first we must consider what Khorenatsi writes in his history, which was completed in AD 474, and was the result of his extensive research.

In the case of Ostan, Khorenatsi has two references; the first is in 1.30 and the second in 2.7. In 1.30 Khorenatsi is writing about the sister of Tigran Sakawakeats (I will not go into the mistaken identity of Tigran in here). He says that "she was sent to live in Tigranocerta", and adds: "They say that the nobility of that region called Ostan had descended from her as a royal line." This statement actually concerns the House of Angeł of south-western Armenia. What is of interest here is the implication of this statement, which makes Ostan much older than all the assertions of both ancient and recent scholars, mentioned above, and, additionally points to a 'House' other than the Arsacids.

Descendants of ancient kings

In 2.7 Khorenatsi returns to the subject of Ostan criticising the state of affairs of his own time. He says that "the actual Ostan consisted of the descendants of the ancient kings of Haykid (true proto-Armenian, progeny of Hayk) origin, and their descendants used to inherit villages and estates . . . but more recently, at the time of the Persian kings, I understand, other sections have been brought into being who call themselves Ostan. I do not know whether this is due to the diminishing numbers of the older generations . . ." And, a sentence later, Khorenatsi insists that "the first Ostan definitely consisted of the descendants of the ancient kings".

Khorenatsi knows that the Arsacids were of Parthian origin, armenicised foreign kings. He would have included them in the Ostan if that was the case. He also knows, but cannot openly say, that the title Ostan was usurped by the Arsacids and others of his own time (he is the bishop of the Bagratids, which forces him to use tact, for fear of appearing to be denouncing the Bagratids, too, as usurpers of an ancient title). As for the Persian kings, Khorenatsi is writing after the fall of the Arsacid kingdom (AD 428), which means, Armenia was largely under the rule of the Persian kings

Khorenatsi makes it clear that Ostan is a title much older than the Arsacids. He does not know exactly how old, but considering that he is writing about Tigran Sakawakeats and the Median king Aždahak, we may deduce that it is the 6th century BC, its members belonging to the ancient 'Houses', most of which do no longer exist; hence his "diminishing numbers".

The conclusion that Ostan is much more ancient than both the Artaxiads and the Arsacids is beyond doubt, which makes it certain that the word could not have derived from either Pahlavi or the Persian language; because it belongs to a time prior to any contacts with these two languages. It must therefore be concluded that Ostan is an indigenous word coming from the proto-Armenian past and describes an exclusive politico-strategic coalition, necessitated by the exigencies of its times.

City-states of the proto-Armenians

Ostan means 'branches', the branches of the proto-Armenians, the city-states of the country of Aram where they had dwelt for 600 years before moving to Armenia. Ostan is also, a convenient term both for the agreements and for the coalition of the proto-Armenians, who were to fight the Medo-Scythian forces in Urartu, and settle in previously agreed parts of the highlands.

Ostan is the compound of 'ost' + 'an'. 'Ost' is an indigenous word, deriving from the Indo-European *ozdos, and means 'branch'; it is related to the Greek 'ozos', German 'ast', Gothic 'asts', Anglo-Saxon 'Ôst', etc. 'An', too, is an indigenous collective suffix and derives from the Indo-European, similar to the English 'en' and 'ne' ('ox' > 'oxen', 'kin' > 'kine', etc.). This 'an' suffix differs from the later Cilician Armenian plural suffix of identical phonetics, which is found only in three cases, such as: 'ji' > 'jian' ['horse']; 'esh' > 'eshan' ['ass'] and 'jori' > 'jorean' ['mule']. The word Ostan has a similar structuring as 'hōr' (< 'hawr') > 'hōran' ('cattle'). The etymology of Ostan is as solid as that of any other indigenous word that derives from ancient Indo-European — there is not a Pahlavi or Persian relationship in this case.

Unfortunately, the meaning of this word had undergone such an unusual change that it became impossible to penetrate the original significance. The reason for the lexical deterioration was due to the exclusive and prestigious character of the word, which could add prestige and grandeur to the name of an up-and-coming new 'family'; even the Arsacids felt the need of such a title in order to enhance their standing.

To trace the birth of the Ostan coalition, and thus of the word, we do not have much to go by. It relates to a proto-Armenian event of the dark ages, which had taken place at a time when there was no Assyria to show interest in what was taking place to the north of its borders, nor was there a Herodotus who might have shown a historian's curiosity. But, we have at our disposal the three name-lists and the observations of Khorenatsi, a few pieces of historical and archaeological evidence, the places where the proto-Armenians had settled in the highlands, and additionally, some proper and place names. Therefore, in order to ascertain who were the original members of the Ostan, and what kind of organization it was, we have to follow Khorenatsi; there are no other sources who throw light on the question, or mention either Ostan or the proto-Armenians' entry into Urartu.

The true Ostan

Khorenatsi in Book I gives us three name-lists of the proto-Armenian rulers. Of these lists, the first is that of the Haykid kings — our subject – the second represents the various branches and the rulers of Aram around 1000-600 BC left out from the first list, and the third is that of the Cilician rulers starting in the 9th century BC, though in Khorenatsi's opinion starting with the non-existent Paroyr Skayorti. Khorenatsi had no part in the compilation of these three name-lists; he had done his research and reported his findings. These he is unable to comprehend, and often gives the wrong explanation, such as the case of Aram and Paroyr.

Khorenatsi remarks that "the true Ostan comprised the descendants of the ancient kings of Haykid origin". In view of this remark, one should thoroughly examine this Haykid list, which at first sight appears faulty, because there are many ancient kings, just as Haykid as any, who are excluded from the list and relegated to the second list, that of the "branches of Aram kingdoms".

For example: the name of Vstamkar (Khelaruada), the father of Gełam (Sulumal); Kaypak (Katuwa), a former king of Garnik (Sangara); Ēndzak (Gunzinanu), a former king of Tork' Angeł (Tarkunazi); Sur (Surri), a former king of Ts'olak (Kulani); these are in addition to the kings of Kummukh and Cilicia who are all missing from the Haykid list. This arbitrary classification of the names as those of Hayk's descendants (they were all true proto-

Armenians) and, particularly, the fact that no one had managed to understand the names and the underlying plan, prompted various scholars to assert that the lists represented a haphazard collection of invented names. Whereas, the ingenuity of the compilation of these name-lists is something much to be admired. We will never know the genius who had compiled them, if they were not the product of centuries of redaction. The Haykid list with its simple structure reveals the names of the true Ostan members, which combined with other data, unravels the history of the conquest of Urartu (if one may call it that), the name of the leading 'House' and the name of the supreme commander of the proto-Armenian forces.

It follows that the composition of these lists and particularly that of the Haykids must have been a deliberate manner of recording oral history, which Khorenatsi was unable to penetrate. In view of the foregoing remarks, the obvious thing to do is to compare the three name-lists Khorenatsi had recorded and find out in what ways they differ from each other. There are two striking differences between the first (Haykid) and the other two name-lists. The first difference, not the most important, is that all the names on this first list represent kingdoms that terminated between 718 and 708 BC. This is why they are called ancient kings. It is true that the second list, too, contains names of kings whose reign came to an end in the same period; but the compiler or compilers had a very good reason for excluding their names from the Haykid list, which brings us to the second difference, the important one.

The second and most important difference between the first and the other two lists lies in the fact that all the names of the first Haykid list have been mentioned in later Armenia either as place names or as patriarchal Houses (later dukedoms). This is irrespective of the fact that some of the correlations between place names and personal names are unacceptable on linguistic grounds. None of the names in the second and third name-lists are to be found, in any form, in later Armenia, which is the reason for their intentional exclusion from the first list.

THE PRE-HISTORY OF THE ARMENIANS

To find out why the survival of the names in later Armenia is so important one must first distinguish the names connected with places from those of patriarchal Houses. The breakdown of the Haykid list gives the following picture — see also the Family Tree of Hayk (p. 150) and the Ostan map (p. 174):

Toponyms

Hayk	Hark' and Haygashen	The Primogenitor
Aramanyak	Aragats mountain	Circuit of Aram country
Aramayis	Armawir city	Great King of Tabal, Tuwatis
Amasia	Masis mountains	Asatuwatimaza of Carchemish
P'arokh	P'arakhod village	Palalam/Larazamasa of Marash
Ts'olak	Ts'olakert village	Kulani of Kinalua (Unqi)
Erast	River Eraskh (Araxi)	Astiruwa of Carchemish
Garnik	Garni city	Sangara of Carchemish
Harma	Father of Aram	Wasusaramimasa of Tabal
Aram	Armenia and Armenians	The country of Aram
Ara the Fair	Plain of Ayrarat	Astiruwa of Carchemish

Patriarchal Houses

Manawaz	Manawazians of Hark'	Muwazisa of Marash (Gurgum)
Khor	Khorkhorunik' (Malkhaz)	Armenicised Hurrians of Carchemish
Baz/Bazuk	Bznunians	Sastura of Carchemish
Kadmos	Kadmeans of the south	Dadi of Khubushkia (Kadmukhi)
Shara	Shahunik' of Sophene	Shakhu/Shadawale of Melid
Shara	Gusharids of the north	Branch of Shakhu/Shadawale
Gełama	Gełark'unik' by Lake Sevan	Sulumal of Melid
Sisak	Sisakan and Sisakeans	Kikki of Tabal
Tork' Angeł	Angeł Tun of Ingilene	Tarkunazi of Melid

The above analysis has given the names of eight patriarchal Houses (number six is of later relevance), which were the original members of the Ostan coalition and the descendants of the ancient Haykid kings. They were all true historical figures as seen in the previous chapter. Additionally, their places of settlement in Armenia, recorded by Khorenatsi, are part of the history of the Armenians. These eight names represent all the proto-Armenian city states of the circuit of Aram (Aramanyak), the country referred to as south-eastern Turkey and northern Syria or the Neo-Hittite kingdoms.[17] I mention below each one of these eight Houses, but we must first deal with Kummukh and Cilicia to see why the names of their ancient rulers were not included in the Haykid list, and why were they not members of the Ostan confederation.

Kummukh

All the kings of Kummukh would have qualified for the first Haykid list as ancient rulers. However, they did not participate in the move to Urartu and were not members of the Ostan confederation, which was the reason for their names appearing in the second list, that of the Aram branches. The proto-Armenians of Kummukh could not join their brethren because Nabuchadrezzar of Babylon had conquered their country in 607 BC.[18] In the previous year, he had annexed some of the lands at the source of the River Tigris, and was busy building fortifications on the lands bordering Urartu.

Cilicia

Khorenatsi's third list does not give us all the names of the rulers of Cilicia, but only a few of them deemed to be important. After the fall of Nineveh, 612 BC, Cilicia Campestris (the eastern half) had become a vassal kingdom of the Medes under Skayorti (son of Ishkallu) and after him under Bačoyč (Syennesis). The principal city of the kingdom was Par (Azatiwata's Pahar — Misis), hence the name of Paroyr (represented as a person by Khorenatsi, due to a misunderstanding), which means "Par to which (kingdom returned)".[19]

Bačoyč had enlarged his domain and at his time Cilicia was at its most prosperous and the only proto-Armenian kingdom then to exist. When the Medo-Lydian hostilities ceased in 585 BC, which was two to three years after the proto-Armenians had entered Urartu, Bačoyč was one of the intermediaries.[20] It is almost certain that the proto-Armenians had taken advantage of Cyaxares's involvement in the west, where the bulk of the Median army was; but the Cilician proto-Armenians could not participate in the enterprise, because of their status of a vassal state and, as things stood, they were doing very well for themselves. The conclusion that they did not participate in the Ostan coalition is therefore well-founded.

The original Ostan houses
Now we must return to the eight original parties of the Ostan coalition, which were: the **Manawazians** of Gurgum (Marash); the **Khorkhorunik'** and the **Bznunians** of Carchemish; the **Shaheans, Gełarkunik'** and **Angeł Tun** of Melid; the **Kadmeans** of Khubushkia (Kadmukhi) and the **Sisakeans** of Tabal. Each one of these 'Houses' has been discussed in the previous chapter, 'The Names of Hayk's Progeny'.

According to what Khorenatsi writes, one can deduce that these eight Houses were all members of the Ostan movement, as they were the descendants of the ancient Haykid kings (the first list). The composition of the first name-list, as seen, highlights these eight Houses, but without mentioning Ostan. However, we know from history the original settlement areas, within Armenia, of these eight Houses, because the districts they had occupied were named after them and continue to be known as such. Therefore, between Khorenatsi, who writes that "the first Ostan was definitely among the descendants of the ancient Haykid kings", the name-list, which is contrived to highlight these eight Haykid ancient Houses and the district names, which are attested by history and are still referred to as such, we have confirmation that Ostan comprised these eight Houses, who put together the original proto-Armenian invading forces that entered Urartu, which action deduced, again, from what Khorenatsi writes, must have taken place in 588-87 BC. There is no other source to confirm this hypothesis or any of its details.

To recapitulate, the places of settlement in the highlands of Armenia of the eight Houses were: the Gełark'unik' commanded the lands to the north-east of the highlands; the Sisakeans to the east; the Kadmeans to the south; the Angeł Tun to the south-west; the Shaheans to the west and a branch of theirs, the Gusharids, to the north (see the Ostan map). Of the central tripartite core, the Bznunians commanded the north-west of Lake Van; the Khorkhorunik' the entire northern coast-lands of the lake; and the Manawazians further to the north of the lake bordering both of these two Houses.

Of all the names mentioned above the House of Manawazians requires a special consideration, because they are rather important for the prehistory of the Armenians. At the end of the 7th century BC the Armenian highlands were still known as Urartu. Within Urartu there was not a family or ex-royal house known as the Manawazian, nor was there a city, their capital, by the name of Mana(wa)zkert (this city might have been the Menuase of the Urartians).

In addition, there could not have been a village by the name of Haykashen nor a Hark' district. The words, which form part of the compounds, seen at the end of each name, such as 'kert' ('build, erect'), 'shen' ('build, erect') and 'Hark'' ('fathers') belong to the Indo-European group of languages and not to a so-called Japhetite (Urartian) dialect. These place names or words and the name of the former royal family of Manawazians (Muwazisa) appear in the highlands after the 6th century BC, that is, after the proto-Armenian move into Urartu.

Every Armenian knows that 'Hark'' means 'fathers' (plural), which can also mean 'begetter, leader, senior, patriarch and director'. The Hark' place name appears in the highlands after the proto-Armenians' arrival, and that, only in the district occupied by the Manawazians, therefore, the title of fathers concerns only the family of Manawazians!

In Khorenatsi's third name-list (1.22), Haykak 'the other' is shown to be a contemporary of Cyaxares, the king of the Medes. We find a village named Haykashen in the Hark' district, which, again, tells us that Haykak (called the second or the other) was the patriarch of the House of Manawazians and that he was the supreme commander of the proto-Armenian forces entering Urartu to fight the Medo-Scythian forces.

The dynasty of Manawazians (the House of Muwazisa of Gurgum) was the oldest proto-Armenian kingdom within the country of Aram, for which they must have been greatly honoured. As a consequence, the various ex-royal Houses of Aram, in the course of their negotiations and eventual agreement, elected the House of Manawazians to head the council or the coalition, and their patriarch to take over the command of the armies.

The dispersion and the places of settlement of the proto-Armenians demonstrates how the circumvention of the highlands was achieved and consequently, the defence of the borders. It also reveals a central governing council consisting from the three most important Houses (in the name-list these three Houses have a special treatment and are shown as the two sons and a grandson of Hayk), who had settled centrally to the north of Lake Van, and headed by the House of the Manawazians.

Power struggles of Cyaxares

The creation of an Ostan coalition could not have happened, had the political situation within the Middle East, and particularly in south-eastern Anatolia, not been conducive. A brief opportunity became available to the proto-Armenians when Cyaxares, the Median king, decided to march on Lydia in 591 BC. After the bloodless conquest of the proto-Armenian city states of Aram, which as Khorenatsi describes in I.13 that "Aram was harassed by the neighbouring nations", Cyaxares had marched to the west and was to be involved in a battle which would continue for six years.

The conjecture that Cyaxares had crossed Urartu in order to march to the west is a fallacy, because the Medians did not subdue Urartu at this particular time; in fact, the kingdom of Urartu, though weakened by internal strife, was still holding its own under Rusa III (610-590 BC). Actually, after this Rusa there was another of the same name, Rusa IV (590-588 BC), who reigned for just two years, according to calculations based on Khorenatsi's writing. The Medo-Lydian hostilities lasted for six years, ending in a stalemate on the 28th of May 585 BC, coinciding with a total eclipse of the sun.

Marching against Lydia, Cyaxares could not afford to leave an Urartu, even a weak one, behind his lines. To thwart any action by Urartu, he had taken the precaution of placing a small army under the leadership of Madyes, son of Bartatua (Protothyes), who with a combined force of Medo-Scythians had already started to subject the people and the country of Urartu to terrible suffering and devastation. From the trilobed arrowheads discovered at Armawir (Argishtikhinili), Bastam (Rusa-patari) and Karmir Blur (Teishebaini) and the level of destruction by fire found in excavations at these cities, in addition to Çavuştepe (Sardurikhinili). Kef-Kalesi and Toprak Kale (Rusakhinili) it can be deduced that the Medo-Scythians,[21] in their efforts to conquer the country had burned and destroyed everything in their path which, up to the time of the proto-Armenian invasion, included the eastern half of the highlands, that is, from Lake Van to the eastern borders.

The Medo-Scythians had also toppled the kingdom of Van (Tushpa, the capital city). Khorenatsi unwittingly confirms these events and additionally gives the full name of the Scythian leader as Niwk'ar Madyes in 1.13, where he writes "Aram (this should be understood as the people of the country of Aram) marched east with 50,000 brave and experienced bowmen and capable lancers, against Madyes, who was leading some Median youths and had already subdued the eastern part of the country, which he held in servitude for two years." No other source gives us any information about this event and period. There are some important revelations in this statement, from which a few valid inferences can be drawn.

Khorenatsi is of the opinion that the country involved was Armenia. We now know that the country would eventually become Armenia, but only after the settlement of the proto-Armenians in its various peripheral districts, which had not then happened. It follows that the country he is referring to was still Urartu. In two years time the hostile forces of the Medo-Scythians under Madyes would manage to conquer the eastern half of the highlands, which is also attested by the archaeological evidence above. This means that Urartu was desperately fighting an unequal war for its independence and survival.

The second revelation is important because it concerns the composition of the hostile army, which we are told was a combined force of Medians and the Scythians (Madyes was the chief of the Scythians after the death of his father). This information settles the argument between scholars, who differ on this issue; one side claiming that it was the Median forces who annihilated Urartu, basing their argument on ceramic finds, whereas the other side says that it was the Scythians, basing their arguments on the trilobed arrow-heads excavated at various sites.[22] It is remarkable that none of these scholars remember the proto-Armenians, who became the masters of the highlands.

The third revelation concerns the direction in which the proto-Armenian forces of the country of Aram marched in order to attack the Medo-Scythian army. Khorenatsi says that "Aram marched to the east" which is certainly correct. The map of south-eastern Anatolia shows that some of the proto-Armenian states, such as Gurgum and Carchemish, were in the south, which makes them to the south-west of Urartu. The forces of these states could not have marched north-east, because Nabuchadrezzar of Babylon had already conquered Kummukh (607 BC) and had started to build fortifications on the lands bordering Urartu. Therefore, Kummukh was impassable, and the proto-Armenians of these southern states had to march first to Melid, regroup, and then advance east to Urartu.

The last point concerns the size of Aram's army and deserves attention. It is a little problematic, because 50,000 fighting men is rather a large number. Cyaxares, after his conquest of the city states of Aram, must have conscripted, for his war against the Lydians, a number of proto-Armenian soldiers according to a historically familiar process, bearing in mind the fact that Aram was a subjugated country of city states with no indigenous rulers. One wonders how such city states without rulers could jointly have raised such a large army other than under the common leadership of the aristocracy from the former royal Houses, who had agreed to cooperate in putting up a combined force.

Once the proto-Armenian forces had crossed into Urartu, this force was to be complemented by the remnants of the Urartian army.

Khorenatsi continues his narrative and writes: "In a surprise dawn attack Aram wiped out the Medo-Scythian forces, captured their leader Niwk'ar, who was called Madyes; taking him to the city of Armawir where he nailed him on to the city wall for all to see."

Nowhere do we notice, or are given the slightest hint of a battle between the proto-Armenians and the Urartians; as for Madyes, we notice, he is not taken to Tushpa (Van), the capital city of Urartu, but to Armawir, the city in Gełark'unik', which was the district most densely populated of the proto-Armenians.

Considering that the Armenians became the masters of the highlands, it has been taken for granted that the proto-Armenians had subdued Urartu. This is another baseless assumption, because at no time did the Armenians either fight with, or subdued Urartu for the mastery of the highlands. In fact, the demise of Urartu belongs to the early years of our own era when the Arsacids had become the rulers of the entire country, which included both Urartu and Armenia, even though the whole country was called Armenia. Urartu remained an independent enclave within Armenia, confined to the east, south-east, south, south-west and the west of Lake Van, which is the main reason for the proto-Armenian settlements on the periphery of the highlands.

It is not possible for a nation to conquer another without seizing the other's capital city. It is a fact that we know nothing about Van/Tushpa of Urartu for over 500 years after the proto-Armenian entry into the country. The first reference to Tushpa/Van is found in the history of Faustos, who is actually writing about events of the fourth century AD, and describes it as "Van, strong city in the district of Tosp" (4.55; 4.59; 5.37). Agathangełos does not mention Tosp at all and Khorenatsi's remarks about "Van of Tosp" also appertains to the 4th century AD.

Urartu versus Aram
Under Darius I (522-486 BC) the highlands were included in the 18th satrapy, which was centred on Tushpa/Van[23] and not the city of Armawir. There is a contradiction in the Behistun inscriptions of c.520 BC. The inscription, in Old Persian, calls the highlands Armenia, but in the Akkadian (Babylonian) version the same highlands are called Urartu. Was it so difficult for the Babylonians to write 'Armina'? We know they had

written the ethnonym of Aramaean whenever they referred to those people. Was there a purpose behind this apparent contradiction? The proto-Armenian places of habitation in the country of Aram, where great numbers of them were to be found, we note were classified as living in the 13th satrapy centred on Melid.[24] This makes it clear that the great number of the proto-Armenians were still in the country of Aram, and those settled on the periphery of the highlands were still at the time a minority compared to the indigenous Urartians.[25]

One might wonder why the Urartians and the proto-Armenians were classified under two different satrapies. The answer may not be to the liking of the Armenian scholars, but from this division it is obvious that the Armenian highlands, although called Armenia, were the home of an independent Urartu under the 18th satrapy, and the country of Aram classified under the city name of Melid was still the home of the independent Armenians.

The Urartians were independent in their own enclave, and were left to take care of their own affairs by the proto-Armenians. Except that, like the proto-Armenians of the periphery of the country they, too, were dominated, first by the Medes and then by the Persians. By that time the coalitions, such as the Ostan, or those of the Urartians of which we know nothing, had no significance and were soon forgotten under the rule of the Persian satrapies.

Herodotus in his *History* (VII.79) testifies that a contingent of the Alarodians (Urartians) served in the Persian army. There was, also, a contingent of Armenians, who were compared to the Phrygians. This separation of the two ethnic groups is also observed by Xenophon, who in Book IV.3 (crossing into Armenia) of his *Persian Expedition* records that at the time of the crossing of the River Centrites (Bohtan Su) the ten thousand were opposed by a force of Armenians, Urartians and Mardians. He adds that "the Chaldaeans (Urartians) are said to be a free nation", which means that in the highlands three separate ethnic groups, at the least, were living side by side, under a Persian satrap.

It is reasonable to expect that certain Urartian and Mardian aristocratic Houses, in their own enclaves, had survived the fall of the Urartian kingdom; Houses such as the Rshtunik', Palunik', Slkunik' and Mardpetakans. These Houses were left undisturbed by the Hays (Armenians), a state of affair, which must have lasted well into the Arsacid era, when the Urartian Houses were recognized and granted dukedoms.

The time Urartu ceased to be an independent enclave was, therefore, in the Arsacid period, when the Armenian language had become dominant in the highlands. By that time the word Ostan had lost its potency and exclusivity. This contributed to the mutation of the word's meaning. By the end of the 4th century AD and nearer to Khorenatsi's own time, only two Houses from the ancient Ostan had survived (the other two in the Byzantine part of Armenia are ignored); the Khorkhorunik' with the title of Malkhaz and the Sisakeans under the new name of Siwnik'. The remarkable thing was that none of these surviving Houses, including those on the Byzantine side, were referred to as Ostan any more, because the title was usurped by the Arsacids and their related minor client dukedoms. These had no knowledge of the actual meaning of the word, but, I am sure, had a full appreciation of its prestige; otherwise, there would have been no point in appropriating it for themselves.

Identifier of a people

It is language that identifies people and nationalities. But, when a language is spoken, within a country, by more than one race for historic reasons, even if they are unrelated, that does not stop the people involved from knowing their different origins, until such time of complete assimilation both linguistically and ethnically.

It appears that the indigenous people of the highlands (Urartians, Mardians, Hurrians, etc.) had always known that

Hayk' (the Armenians) were migrant interlopers, which in mid-Arsacid era gave rise to a certain collusion between the Arsacid kings and the remnants of the leading Urartian Houses, when the Haykid aristocracy such as the Manawazians, Ortunis, Bznunians, etc. were being wiped out. The Khorkhorunik' of the original Ostan coalition survived because they were not of true proto-Armenian origin.

The whole affair appears to have been planned for the benefit of the indigenous Urartians, which is self-evident from the high offices they attained, and yet, it was Urartu that sometime after the accession of Rusa IV, in perhaps, 589 BC, had asked for proto-Armenian help and had agreed to share their lands.

The conclusion is inescapable that there must have been such an agreement whereby the division of the country was decided. The Urartu–proto-Armenian agreement was the origin of the birth of the Ostan coalition, and it is practically certain that the remnants of the Urartian army joined forces with the proto-Armenians in the fight against the Medo-Scythian agressors. The strongest, and indeed undeniable, support for such a conclusion comes from the places of settlement of the proto-Armenians on the periphery of the highlands. It is also evident that the result of this agreement between the Urartians and the proto-Armenians was the complete separation of the two races, and, of course, the isolation of the Urartians in their enclave for the next 500 years at least.

It is remarkable that even the later proto-Armenian migrations, both from the Balkans and Anatolia, never encroached on the lands allocated to the Urartians. They settled, again, in places on the periphery of the highlands, such as the Odomantians who settled to the west, in Lesser Sophene; the Gordyene and the Mygdonians who settled to the extreme south of the highlands around Nisibis. In other words, the proto-Armenians stuck to the letter of their agreement.

Khorenatsi says that "Hayk found some people already dwelling on the lands he settled in, and these were the first to submit and, of course, to assimilate" (Book 1.12).

The Urartians, encircled by the proto-Armenians on all sides were unable to sustain full contact with the outside world.[26] Thus, when bilingualism started to penetrate slowly to the core of their enclave, it proved disastrous for them. Whereas, the proto-Armenian language was receiving fresh impetus all the time from the arrival of wave after wave of their kin, either from the Balkans or from Anatolia, the Urartian language was fading away in line with their identity. The eclipse of the Urartian language was the reason for Urartu, as a separate ethnic unit, to die a natural death; but even that death could not negate the legacy with which Urartu had endowed the hybrid nation of the Armenians, who are while physiognomically of Caucasian type, yet speak an Indo-European dialect.

NOTES

Introduction and Part One

1. These two ethnic units are the most important of the hybridisation. There were also other ethnic minorities, who in time assimilated, such as the Mardians, Hurrians, Kaska, Urumeans, Hittites, Aramaeans, etc. In fact, up to the 5th century AD there were 19 different languages spoken in the highlands. H. Adjaryan, *The History of the Armenian Language*, State University, Erevan, 1940. See vol. I, chapter 9.
2. This assertion is based on what Movses Khorenatsi says in his *History of the Armenians*. He is the only historian that gives a true account of the period and the events.
3. The appellation Armenian was originally attached to the Indo-European newcomers, the Hays. It was much later that the other ethnic groups, too, were called Armenians.
4. D. M. Lang, *Armenia: Cradle of Civilization*, George Allen & Unwin, 1970. Lang's remarks on p. 37, I am sure, have in mind the Classical Armenian language, because he could not have known about the proto-Armenians.
5. Ibid. p. 38.
6. See the following works in English, from which I have benefited: R. D. Barnett, 'Urartu' in *Cambridge Ancient*

History, vol. III, part 1, 1982. B. B. Piotrovsky, *Urartu, the Kingdom of Van and its Art*, Evelyn Adams & Mackay, London, 1967. Idem, *Urartu*, Nigel Publishers, Geneva, 1969. E. Ungar, 'Urartu', in M. Ebert (ed.), *Reallexikon der Vorgeschichte*, XIV, 32, Berlin.

7.   The Mkhit'arian Monastery on the island of St Lazzaro, Venice, has been, since its foundation, one of the most important centres of Armenian studies.

8.   Chamchian, Michael, *The History of the Armenians*, 1784-86, Venice.

9.   Movses Khorenatsi, *The History of the Armenians*, translated from the classical Armenian to the modern by S. Malkhazyants, Erevan, 1940. This work is available in English, translated by R. W. Thomson, Harvard University Press, 1978, and in French by A. and J.-P. Mahé, Gallimard, 1993.

10.   Genesis, 10:2-4.

11.   Josephus, Flavius, *The Antiquities of the Jews*, Pickering & Inglis, London 1960. See book I, ch. VI.1, where it is stated: "Thiras also called those whom he ruled over, Thirasians; but the Greeks changed the name into Thracian."

12.   The first inscribed evidence of this appears in the trilingual inscription of Darius of circa 520 BC. However, the appellation Arminā must have derived from the Aramaean Armināiā, which must have been in use before Darius's own time.

13.   Byzantinus, Stephanus, *Ethnica*, ed. W. Dindorf, Leipzig, 1825. I. L. Merker, 'The Ancient Kingdom of Paeonia', *Balkan Studies*, 6/1, 1965.

14.   Strabo, *Geography*, Loeb Classical Series, Harvard University Press, 1989 reprint. See II.14.12 — Strabo does not mention Seleucus Nikator. He says that the two historians accompanied Alexander the Great. Seleucus (312-280 BC) was the inheritor of the Near Eastern and the Asian lands.

15.   According to Strabo (II.4.8), Armenus was a native of

NOTES

Armenium, one of the cities on Lake Boebeïs, between Phrae and Larissa, hence his name. Anania Shirakatsi, a 7th century AD philisopher in Armenia, in his *Ashkharatsoyts (Geography)*, p. 274 of the 1973 edition, mentions the "Great Thessaly as the country from where the Armenians (Hayk') came".

16. Apollonius of Rhodes in his *Voyage of the Argo* (Penguin Classics, reprint 1983), does not mention such a name as one of the Argonauts.

17. Strabo, *Geography*, frag. VII.38.

18. R. A. Crossland, 'Linguistic Problems of the Balkan Area, in late prehistoric and early Classical Period', in *Cambridge Ancient History*, vol. III, part 1, 1982: chap. 20c.

19. V. I. Georgieve, LB, I, 1959b; LB, 2, 1960. P. Kreischmer, H. Krahe, A. Mayer and D. Detschew agree with his opinion (in Djahukyan, see following note).

20. G. B. Djahukyan, *The History of the Armenian Language: the Pre-literate Period*, (in Armenian), Erevan, 1987 — part II, II, A.3 (p. 282).

21. Ibid.

22. O. R. Gurney, *The Hittites*, 1952. J. Lehman, *The Hittites*, 1977.

23. D. M. Lang, *Armenia: Cradle of Civilization*, 1970 — pp. 78-9.

24. H. Adjaryan, *Dictionary of Armenian Root Words*, Erevan 1971-79, 4 vols.

25. After the proto-Armenian entry into Urartu, the east, south and west of Lake Van were left to the indigenous Urartians as their own lands within Armenia.

26. On the border of the Hittites, adjoining Khayasha, there used to be a city named Ura, which Armenian scholars considered to be a city of the Urumeans; whereas the Tiglath-Pileser I inscription points to the west as the place from where these people came from and calls them "unruly Hittites".

Eremyan's and Łapantsyan's assertions are not acceptable.

27.   D. D. Lukenbill, *Ancient Records of Assyria and Babylonia* — the Annals (366) and the Broken Obelisk inscription 389-91, concerning Adad-nirari II.

28.   I. M. Diakonoff, *The Prehistory of the Armenian People*, English edition by Caravan Books, N.Y., 1984. See note 151, p. 166.

29.   G. B. Djahukyan, 'The Hayassan Language and its relation to the Indo-European Languages', in *Archiv Orientalni*, 29, 2, 1961. Diakonoff maintains that Djahukyan's opinion based on restructured Indo-European stems is arbitrary.

30.   Lang, *Armenia: Cradle of Civilization*.

31.   Diakonoff, *The Prehistory of the Armenian People*.

32.   V. V. Ivanov and T. V. Gamkrelidze in Diakonoff's *The Prehistory of the Armenian People*. See notes 35 (p. 135), 9 (p146) and 7 (p. 205) of Diakonoff's history.

33.   J. P. Mallory, *In Search of the Indo-Europeans*, Thames & Hudson, London, 1989 (paperback ed. 1996) — p. 182.

34.   Djahukyan, *The History of the Armenian Language*.

35.   Diakonoff, *The Prehistory of the Armenian People*. On p 205 he remarks that "the paper written by Ivanov and Gamkrelidze (1981) raises grave doubts. It is based on inconclusive data from various languages with a disregard of historical and geographical conditions."

36.   Gurney, *The Hittites*, chapter IX — 'Art, some problems' (p. 213).

37.   Diakonoff, *The Prehistory of the Armenian People*.

38.   In this connection it is worthwhile to mention the Arimean Mountains of the Iliad (II.907). The whole quotation is so ambiguous that each scholar has formed his own individual opinion. Whatever the explanation (some point to Cilicia as the place), it is certain that the word 'Arimean' cannot be correlated with the ethnonym Armenian of the 6th century BC.

39. R. A. Crossland, 'Linguistic Problems of the Balkan Area, in late prehistoric and early classical period', in Cambridge Ancient History, vol. III, part I, 1982.
40. Shirakatsi, Anania, *Ashkharatoyts* (*Geography*).
41. Maximus of Tyre, *Philisophoumena*, 2.8, 6 quoted by R. Vasič in "Bronzes from Titov Veles (the Paeonian Bylazora) in the Benaki Museum" in *Živa Antika*, 24 (1974b). See also John Wilkes, *The Illyrians*, Blackwell, Oxford, 1992, p. 244.
42. Ivan Pudič, 'Indo-European Mythology in the Bronze Age', in *Bronze Age Migrations in the Aegean: Proceedings of the First International Colloquium on the Aegean Prehistory*, Sheffield, 1, 1974.
43. Ibid — note that after Urartu was named Armenia, the country became a satrapy, therefore, under the influence of the Achamaenids. Under these new circumstances Thyales was discarded and forgotten, but his orgasmic aspects were conferred onto the newly adopted goddess Anahida.
44. Hieroglyphic inscription TOPADA, line 5, of Wasusaramimasa (Harma), published in my next study, *The Pre-history of the Armenians Volume 2 — The Proto-Armenian Hieroglyphic Inscriptions of Aram* (Bennett and Bloom, 2003), is of great interest in this connection, and reads: "NA ti ia+ra PRIEST ASANA HUR wa tá wa mu tá TARA MOON-mi zi" = "prior to attacking the priests raised fire so that I offer prayers to the Moon."
45. Ivan Pudič, 'Indo-European Mythology in the Bronze Age'. Note that, the Teutonic god of war Tiw (Greek Ares, Roman Mars) was also known as Tyr, which may have some implications regarding the original place from where the proto Armenians/Paeonians came to the Balkans, particularly, when there are Teutonic, Baltic and Finno-Ugric loan words in the Armenian language. However, the Scandinavian great god Odin of wisdom, magic, ecstasy, gaining wealth, poetry and war, appears to have attributes which are closer to the Armenian/

Paeonian Tyr. Nevertheless, some scholars have ascribed to Tyr an Iranian derivation and compared it with Tishtrya, a minor and rather obscure god!

46. Michael Grant, *The Rise of the Greeks*, Weidenfield & Nicolson, London, 1987 — chapter 1.

47. Djahukyan, *The History of the Armenian Language*, part II.II.2-3.

48. *Dictionary of Religion*, Penguin, pp. 123 and 132.

49. N. G. L. Hammond, 'Illyris, Epirus and Macedonia in the Early Iron Age', in *Cambridge Ancient History*, vol. III, part 1 (1982). See chapter 15, p. 630.

50. Lord Derby's translation of the *Iliad*, Everyman's Library, 1948.

51. Herodotus, V.1.

52. Khorenatsi, who mentions the name of Zarmayr for the first time, had benefited from Diodorus's story of the Trojan War through the *Chronicon* of Eusebius. Diodorus or Eusebius do not mention the name of Pyraechmes, neither that of Zarmayr. It is a mystery where Khorenatsi had found this name, because the name is the only part of his narrative that correlates with the story in the *Iliad*.

53. Thucydides, II.96

54. Strabo, II.14.2

55. Herodotus, V.15

56. Strabo, 12.3.9

57. Herodotus, V.15, and Strabo, VII.36

58. Herodotus, V.15

59. Strabo, VII.38-41

60. *Armenian Encyclopaedia*, Erevan 1974 — see vol. II, pp. 262-63.

61. Irwin L. Merker, 'The Ancient Kingdom of Paeonia', in *Balkan Studies*, 6/1, 1965.

62. Plutarch, *Lives*, 'Alexander', Everyman's Library, 1910.

63. Merker, 'The Ancient Kingdom of Paeonia'.

64. Ibid.

65. Pausanias, *Description of Greece*, vol. IV, book X, xiii, no.1, Loeb Classical Library, 1995.
66. Merker, 'The Ancient Kingdom of Paeonia'.
67. N. K. Sandars, *The Sea People: Warriors of the Ancient Mediterranean*, Thames & Hudson, London, 1978.
68. R. D. Barnett, 'The Sea People', in *Cambridge Ancient History*, vol. II, part 2, 1978 — ch. 18, iv.
69. T. & M. Dothan, *People of the Sea*, McMillan, N.Y., 1992. See also A. R. Burn, *Minoans, Philistines and Greeks*, K. Paul Trench Trubner, London, 1930.
70. To support this assertion, we have the names of the rulers and their inscriptions in the proto-Armenian language, published in my *The Pre-History of the Armenians Volume 2*.
71. A. K. Grayson, *Assyrian Royal Inscriptions*, vol. II, no. 12 (162), 172-176. This conclusion derives from the inscription of Tiglath Pileser I, who is the first to mention these people. It appears Diakonoff agrees with this view.
72. According to the inscription of Tiglath-Pileser, the Urumeans together with the Kaskans came from the west, for which they are referred to as Hittites. The Uru/Ura stem of the name of Urumean is found mainly in west Anatolia (Lycia, Lyddia) — see Ph. H. J. Houwink Ten Cate, *The Luwian Population Groups* (Brill, 1961), which is the basis of my assertion that the Urumeans spoke a dialect of Luwian. Furthermore, the presence of a Luwian-speaking group in the highlands will account for the Luwian loan words in the Armenian language.
73. Gurney, *The Hittites*.
74. Grayson, *Assyrian Royal Inscriptions*.
75. These two ethnonyms of Phrygian and Mysian are attested by the appellation of Mushki (proto-Armenian Musaka) for the Phrygians, and the name of the city of Mush, to the west of Lake Van, for the Mysians (proto-Armenian Musa). See also Crossland, note 18 above.
76. Homer, *The Iliad*, Book XXI, 169-178.

77. Diakonoff, *The Prehistory of the Armenian People* — ch. 3.2.4.

78. The Carians, in ancient works, were identified with the Leleges and were linked to the Lycians; but Strabo differentiates them from both the Leleges and the Lycians (Strabo 7.7.2; 12.8.7; 13.1.58). Unfortunately the excavations at Bayraklı have thrown no light on the matter.

79. Strabo, 12.3.20

80. J. A. Wilson, 'VI Egyptian Historical Texts', *Anet*, pp. 262-63.

81. It is plausible that the Egyptian 'RWKW' can be equated with the inhabitants of the Hittite 'Lukka Lands', located to the south-west of Anatolia. The Egyptians and the Hittites knew these people since the 14th century BC. They were also one of the members of the Libyan alliance at the time of Merneptah of Egypt.

82. Wilson, 'VI Egyptian Historical Texts'.

83. Grayson, *Assyrian Royal Inscriptions*.

84. Houwink Ten Cate, *The Luwian Population Groups*. The later name of this city, to the west of Cilicia, was Olba.

85. Diakonoff, *The Prehistory of the Armenian People* — note 151, p. 166.

86. Djahukyan, *The History of the Armenian Language*, part II.II.4.

87. Grayson, *Assyrian Royal Inscriptions*.

88. Ibid.

89. Hieroglyphic inscription Carchemish, A 6.3 of Yarairaisa.

90. The name of the city of Mush confirms that the Mysians were one of the members of the coalition. See Crossland (note 18 above) — chapter 20c, iv (p. 849).

91. Diakonoff, *The Prehistory of the Armenian People* — see 3.2.4 and 3.2.24.

92. Gurney, *The Hittites*, chapter 1.3 (p. 39) where the name of Mita appears. Toumanoff and Lang base their theory of the Armenian ethnogenesis on this single name and make

the Armenian language a mixture of Khayashan and Phrygian languages. Djahukyan says that the old Phrygian and the Armenian languages were closely affined, which may have a historical explanation, because the two nations have been neighbours for at least a thousand years.

93. R. D. Barnett, 'Karatepe, the Key to the Hittite Hieroglyphics', in *Anatolian Studies*, 3, 1953, p. 66.

94. J. D. Hawkins, 'The Neo-Hittite States in Syria and Anatolia', in *Cambridge Ancient History*, vol. III, part 1 (1982), p 372 ('Introduction').

95. Diakonoff, *The Prehistory of the Armenian People*, ch. 1.22.5 (p. 20). See also A. Göetze, 'The Cilicians', in *Journal of Cuneiform Studies*, 16, 1962; and Gurney, *The Hittites*, '3. The Empire', p. 26.

96. Wilson, 'VI Egyptian Historical Texts'.

97. Hawkins, 'The Neo-Hittite States in Syria and Anatolia'.

98. Göetze, 'The Cilicians'.

99. Ibid.

100. Barnett, 'Karatepe, The Key to Hittite Hieroglyphs'.

101. Ibid.

102. Hawkins, "The Neo-Hittite States in Syria and Anatolia"

103. P. Kreischmer and H. Krahe in *Homerische Personennamen — Sprachwissenschaftliche und historische Klassifikation*, ed. H. von Kamptz, Göttinger, 1982, p. 330.

104. Radoslav Katičič, *Ancient Languages of the Balkans*, Mouton de Gruyter, 1977.

105. Herodotus, V.17; V.98.

106. Merker, 'The Ancient Kingdom of Paeonia'.

107. Plutarch, *Lives*, 'Alexander', vol. II. p. 498.

108. N. G. L. Hammond, *The Miracle that was Macedonia*, Sidgwick and Jackson, 1991, p. 143.

109. Merker, 'The Ancient Kingdom of Paeonia'.

110. Katičič, *Ancient Languages of the Balkans*.

111. Barnett, 'The Sea People' — see note 68 above.

112. Kreischmer and Krahe — see note 103 above.

113. Lukenbill, *Ancient Records of Assyria*.

114. Merker, 'The Ancient Kingdom of Paeonia'.

115. H. P'asdermačian, *The History of the Armenians*, (trans. M. Ishkhan), Hamazgain Armenian Cultural Association (no. 10), Beirut, 1980, p. 41.

116. Adjaryan, *History of the Armenian Language*, vol. II, p.127.

117. Plutarch, *Lives*, 'Alexander'.

118. Ibid.

119. Merker, 'The Ancient Kingdom of Paeonia'.

120. Ibid.

121. Kreischmer and Krahe — see note 103 above.

122. Katičič, *Ancient Languages of the Balkans*.

Part Two

1. The inscription of Suhis I, Carchemish A 1a, line 2 (Hawkins's sentence nos. 12-13), records the following: "awa Haza-u-nana CITY arha TU+ra haha za ha; PI na pawa mu za na χa-a ha si+na", which translates as: After (awa) the Hay People (Hayu nana) of the city (city arha) by force (tura) pacified them (haha za ha) provisions (pi na) I gave them (pawa mu za na) to eliminate (sina ha) destitution (χa-a). Note that the ancient word 'tura' means sword, therefore, 'by sword' was translated as 'by force'.

2. J. D. Hawkins, 'Building Inscriptions of Carchemish', in *Anatolian Studies*, 22, 1972. See pp. 88-89, sentence 12.

3. A. K. Grayson, *Assyrian Royal Inscriptions*, vol. 2. Ashurnasirpal II, 584. iii 56.

4. D. D. Lukenbill, *Ancient Records of Assyria*, Shalmaneser III, year 1, 'II: The Monolith Inscription', col. I.1.29-II.1.13.

5. Scholarship has failed to read this name. Meriggi reads as: LA-x-ma-sa-a-s; and Hawkins reads as: LA+_-ma-s and Laramas.

NOTES

6. Lukenbill, *Ancient Records of Assyria*, 'II: The Monolith Inscription' — see note 4 above.
7. Ibid., 6th year, col. II, 78-102.
8. J. D. Hawkins, 'Assyrians and Hittites', in *Iraq*, 36, 1974. pp. 733-75.
9. D. D. Lukenbill, *Ancient Records of Assyria*, 'Inscriptions of Tiglath-Pileser III', The Annals, year 3 (769).
10. A. G. Lie, *The Inscriptions of Sargon II, King of Assyria*, Libraire Orientaliste Paul Geuthner, Paris, 1929. The Annals, 11th year (234; 1-5).
11. I. M. Diakonoff, *The Prehistory of the Armenian People*, ch. 2.3.13, pp. 93-6.
12. Kreischmer and Krahe — see note 103 for Chapter one.
13. R. D. Barnett, 'Urartu', in *Cambridge Ancient History*, Vol.III, part 1, 1982. p. 343.
14. Ibid., p. 349.
15. Diakonoff, *The Prehistory of the Armenian People*, ch. 2.3.6, p. 85.
16. Ibid., note 229, pp. 172-73.
17. J. D. Hawkins, 'The Neo-Hittite States in Syria and Anatolia', *Cambridge Ancient History*, vol. III., part 1, p. 419.
18. Lie, The Inscriptions of Sargon II, King of Assyria, pp. 205-206.
19. Ibid., p. 208.
20. Ibid., pp. 210-213.
21. Ibid., pp. 212-213
22. Ibid., p. 221
23. Ibid., pp. 209
24. Hawkins, 'The Neo-Hittite States in Syria and Anatolia', p. 428.
25. Ibid.
26. Lukenbill, *Ancient Records of Assyria*, 781.
27. R. Campbell Thompson and M. E. L. Mallowan, *The British Museum Excavation at Nineveh*, 'Inscriptions of

Ashurbanipal from the Temple of Ishta', 138-45.

28. J. D. Hawkins, 'Hieroglyphic Hittite Inscriptions of Commagene', in *Anatolian Studies*, 20, 1970.

29. Seton Lloyd, *Ancient Turkey*, 1989. Chapter 7, p. 73.

30. Khorenatsi refers to this place in the plural as cemeteries, even though Eshpai (Hayk) buried only one person, Sargon II. Khorenatsi's statement is contradictory, unless the place was already known as cemeteries and all Hayk did was to repeat an established procedure.

31. J. D. Hawkins, "The Neo-Hittite States in Syria and Anatolia", p. 389

32. H. Adjaryan, *Dictionary of Armenian Personal Names* (Erevan, 1972) and *Dictionary of Armenian Root Words* (Erevan, 1971-79). Both of these works discuss these names and their derivation.

33. Adjaryan, *Dictionary of Armenian Root Words* — see under 'Eš'.

34. I. F. Gelb, *Hurrians and Subarians*, University of Chicago Press, 1944.

35. Gurney, *The Hittites*.

36. D. D. Lukenbill, *Ancient Records of Assyria and Babylonia*, Chicago, 1926-7 — Shalmaneser, 6th year (610).

37. Hawkins, 'Assyrians and Hittites', *Iraq*, 36, 1974.

38. Ibid.

39. Ibid.

40. Lukenbill, *Ancient Records of Assyria and Babylonia* — Tiglath-Pileser, 3rd year (769).

41. A. G. Lie, *The Inscriptions of Sargon I, King of Assyria*, Paris, 1929.

42. Ibid.

43. Ibid., 415-416.

44. J. D. Hawkins, 'Some Historical Problems of the Hieroglyphic Luwian Inscriptions', *Anatolian Studies*, 19, 1979, p. 163.

45. Hawkins, 'The Neo-Hittite States in Syria and Anatolia'.

46. Adjaryan, *Dictionary of Armenian Personal Names*.
47. Hawkins, 'Some Historical Problems…', as in note 44 above. P. Meriggi, *Manuale di Eteo Geroglifico*, Roma 1967, p. 123, sentence 2.
48. Lukenbill, *Ancient Records of Assyria and Babylonia*, (801).
49. Adjaryan, *Dictionary of Armenian Root Words* — see 'Hoy'.
50. Lukenbill, *Ancient Records of Assyria and Babylonia*, (802).
51. A. G. Lie, *The Inscriptions of Sargon II, King of Assyria*, pp. 194-197.
52. Ibid., pp. 198-199.
53. Ibid., pp. 203-204.
54. Hawkins, 'The Neo-Hittite States in Syria and Anatolia'.
55. Ibid.
56. J. N. Postgate, 'Assyrian Texts and Fragments', *Iraq*, 35, 1973.
57. Hawkins, 'The Neo-Hittite States in Syria and Anatolia'.
58. A. Göetze, 'The Cilicians', *Journal of Cuneiform Studies*, 16, 1962.
59. Houwink Ten Cate, *The Luwian Population Groups*.
60. A. K. Grayson, *Assyrian and Babylonian Chronicles — Texts from Cuneiform Sources*, Locust Valley, N. Y., 1975 — Chronicle 1,7-8.
61. Lukenbill, *Ancient Records of Assyria and Babylonia*, (782).

Part Three

1. In pre-literate Armenia economic and political archives did exist, but these were in Greek, Aramaean and Old Persian, as testified by Khorenatsi, Book I.3.
2. Seton Lloyd, *Ancient Turkey*, 1989.
3. Grayson, *Assyrian and Babylonian Chronicles*.
4. R. Campbell Thompson and M. E. L. Mallowan, *Annals of Archaeology and Anthropology* — 'The inscription of Ashurbanipal from the Temple of Ishtar', p. 96.

5.   C. Toumanoff, *Studies in Christian Caucasian History*, Georgetown University Press, 1963. Toumanoff examines the various Houses of Armenia and discusses the opinions of many scholars. But his study suffers from contradictions and contains too many conjectures in the case of the Armenian ethnogenesis, the ethnicity of the Orontids and many of the dukedoms. According to Toumanoff the dukedoms comprised thirteen Houses of Orontids, ten of Arsacids, five of Urartians, four of Mihranids, four of Medo-Mannaeans, two of Mardians, and one each of Alban, Canaanite, Georgian, Hurrian, Kaska, Pala and Sala. One wonders whether there were any Armenians (Hays) in Armenia? As for the important subject of Ostan, it appears, many have discussed it but none show an understanding of what it exactly was.

6.   Ibid., p. 208.

7.   Justinian 4.1-2. (Reference taken from Chamchian's *The History of the Armenians*)

8.   Hawkins, 'Assyrians and Hittites', *Iraq*, 36, 1974 — see pp. 73-75.

9.   Toumanoff on p. 332 of his *Studies in Christian Caucasian History*, and R. W. Thomson on page 58 of his translation of Khorenatsi's *History of the Armenians*, claim that the name Sisakan was first mentioned by a Syriac named Zacharias Rhetor of AD 554. If one accepts such a claim, then the name Sisakan would be a well kept secret in Armenia and it would take a foreign scholar to enlighten the Armenians. Furthermore, the two academics mentioned offer no explanation as to how Zacharias's works became available to the Armenians of the fifth century AD, a century before the time of this Syriac. See also note 12 below.

10.   Flavius Josephus, *Antiquities of the Jews*, book I, chapter VI.4.

11.   G. J. Gadd, in *Cambridge Ancient History*, vol. V, chapter 19. The inscription reads: "Naram-Sin, king of the four

regions, when he wared against Khurshamatki, lord of Aram and Am, in Tibar, the mountain, he overcame him." (Khurshamatki is a Hurrian name.)

12.   Koryun, *Life of Mashtots*, ed. 1962. — chapter 7, p. 100.

13.   Aratus, 402-410. Loeb Cl. Library, trans. G. R. Mair, 1921. How the Armenians got hold of this information in the fifth century AD is a puzzle. Aratus was not translated into Armenian, therefore the information may be a later addition.

14.   This definition of the word is based on the fact that Khel of Khelaruada has been translated as 'vest' in the recomposition of the name – vest means noble.

15.   The anonymous history attributed to Sebēos is an important document because the author describes events of his own and near to his own time starting with chapter seven. However, there are six more chapters as the beginning of the history, which aspire to recount a complete prehistory of the Armenians. Of these chapters number one is the most enigmatic and misunderstood and tends to lend itself to improvements and adulteration, which we see in the publications of Patkanian of 1879 and Abgaryan of 1965. Chapter one starts with a declaration, a prologue, wherein the author admits that he is not an experienced researcher and chronicler, but acceding to the request of his patron (not named) he will record: a) the legendary history of the ancient heros; b) the history of what happened since those times; and c) the history of the disasters of his own time, which took place during the reign of five kings. The author is, more or less, successful in fulfilling his promise. But his chapter one is naive, incoherent and in places contradictory — because it is written from memory of what he had read in his youth. Some of the subjects he mentions are not found in Khorenatsi's history, from which he has taken the interesting and easier to remember stories of Hayk and Bel and Ara the Fair and Semiramis. But even in these cases he

imprints his own ideas onto the stories, such as the exchange of words between Hayk and Bel in the course of their battle, etc. For the benefit of the reader I should mention that chapter one has sufficient material for one to date it to the seventh century AD, which has escaped the attention of scholars who have shown interest in this history.

16. There was an Angł castle in the Tzałkots district of central Armenia. It appears scholars want to create another, I do not know for what purpose.

17. J. D. Hawkins, 'The Neo-Hittite States in Syria and Anatolia'.

18. A. K. Grayson, 'Babylonian Chronicles No.4' — Nabopolassar, lines 13-15.

19. Khorenatsi, *The History of the Armenians*. In Book I.21, he writes about Skayordi and Paroyr, saying: "Or i Skayordwoyn Paroyr' arajin i Hays t'agaworē", which Malkhazyants has translated as "Born to Skayordi Paroyr who for the first time reigned in Armenia". Thomson translates the same sentence as "Paroyr, son of Skayordi, was the first to reign in Armenia". Khorenatsi's sentence literally translated says: "About Skayordi from whom Par-to-which, first reigns over Armenians" ('i Hays' means both Armenia and Armenians). Both scholars mentioned have understood this ambiguous and contradictory sentence in the way Khorenatsi believes it to be true. It appears Khorenatsi has gathered information about Skayordi which he does not really understand. Therefore, he makes Paroyr a person and the son of Skayordi — the same statement is repeated two more times further down the chapter. There has never been a person by the name of Paroyr in the prehistory of the Hays; Paroyr is a compound of Par+oyr, meaning 'Par to which'. The person who was advanced by Cyaxares to the status of a vassal king was Skayordi. The city he was to reign over was Par (appears in Azatiwata's Karatepe Inscription, sentence VII, as Pahar — Misis).

Khorenatsi's sentence is contradictory, because Paroyr could not be "the first to reign in Armenia". He had recorded the names of some forty odd kings before Paroyr, as the Haykids or as kings after Aram. The sentence should have said "Skayordi was the first to reign over the Armenians of Par city (in Cilicia)". Now, if one is to say "Born to Argishti Erebuni", or adapting Thomson's style of translation, "Erebuni, son of Argishti", one with a little knowledge of the Urartian history would understand the message that the city of Erebuni was founded by Argishti. The situation, in the case of Skayordi and Paroyr, is identical, except that Khorenatsi does not understand it and accepts the information as literally true. He had done the same in the cases of Aramanyak, Kadmos and Aram.

20. Herodotus, Book I. 173-4. Bačoyč (Syennesis) must have been the son of Skayordi as he is the next king to rule over Par (Misis). He was a successful king who enlarged his domain and eventually became the ruler of the whole of Cilicia Campestris.

21. Barnett, *Urartu*.

22. Ibid.

23. Herodotus, Book III.94 and VII.79.

24. Ibid.

25. Diakonoff, *The History of The Armenian People* — see Chapter III.3.1.

26. This inability to sustain full contact with the outside world was the main reason the outside world forgot Urartu and its achievements, which can be seen in the fact that no historian or writer of any country wrote about the people of Urartu. And the records that existed in cuneiform inscriptions, spread about the highlands, were completely overlooked until the 18th century. There are some minor references in the Bible, Herodotus, Xenophon, Josephus, etc., but these do not tell us much.

SYNCHRONISTIC LIST OF PROTO-ARMENIAN RULERS

Circa	CARCHEMISH	GURGUM (Marash)	MELID (Malatya)	KUMMUKH
1000				
	†Suhis I (Yoys I)	†Larazamasa (P'arokh I)		
	†Asatuwatimaza (Amasia)	Muwazisa (Manawaz)		
950				
	†Suhis II (Yoys II)	Halparutiya I (Hrand I)		
	†Katuwa (Kaypak)			
900		Muwazali (Arbown)		
	Sangara (Garnik)	†Halparutiya II (Hrand II)		Qatazilu (Ampak)
850				Kundashpi (Vashtak)
		Larazamasa II (P'arokh II)		
		†Halparutiya III (Hrand III)		†Panamuwatis/ Ushpilulume
800			Shakhu/Shadawale (Shara)	
	Astiruwa (Erast) †Yarairaisa (Arayan Ara) †Kamana (Hawanak)		Khelaruada (Vstamkar)	Kushtashpi (Shawarsh)
750	Sastura (Baz)	Tarkulara	Sulumal (Gełama)	
	†Pisiris (Husak)		Gunzinanu (Ĕndzak)	
		Mutallu (Arbown)	Tarkanazi (Tork-Angeł)	Mutallu (Arbown)
700			Mugallu (Mshak)	
650			...ussi (Anowshavan)	

SYNCHRONISTIC LIST OF PROTO-ARMENIAN RULERS

Circa	TABAL	TABAL DISCTRICTS	CILCIA AND DISTRICTS	UNQI (Patinu)
900				
			Pikhirim of Kilakku (P'arnawaz) Kate of Que	
850	Tuatte (T'agat) **Kikki (Sisak)**	Pukhamme of Khubishna	Kirrie of Que Tulli of Tanakun	**Surri** (Sowr)
800	**Tuwatis (Aramayis)** †Ruwas, advisor			
750	†**Wasusaramimasa** (Harma)	**Uirimme** (Perč) Tukhamme of Ishtunda Ushkhitti of Atuna	†**Azatıwata** (Norayr)	**Kulani** (Ts'olak)
	Khully (Hoy)	**Kiakki of Shinukhtu** (Głak) **Kurti of Atuna** (Kornak)		
	Ambaris			
700	**Ishkallu** (Ska) **Mugallu** (Mshak)	**Gurti of Togarmah** (Gorak)	Kirua of Illubru **Sanduarri of Sissu & Kundu** (Arnak) **Sandasarme of Khilakku** (Hhrachia) **Syennesis** (Pačoyč) **Appuwashu** (Baros)	

NOTES

1. All the names in bold have been recorded by Movses Khorenats'i in his *History of the Armenians*, book I.
2. Names marked † are those who have left behind their own inscriptions.

INDEX